THE STOOGE FAN'S I.Q. TEST

THE STOOGE FAN'S I.Q. TEST

THE ULTIMATE CHALLENGE!

Ronald L. Smith

CONTEMPORARY
BOOKS

CHICAGO · NEW YORK

Library of Congress Cataloging-in-Publication Data

Smith, Ronald L., 1952–
    The Stooge fan's IQ test : the ultimate challenge / Ronald L.
Smith.
        p.   cm.
    ISBN 0-8092-4613-9 (pbk.) : $6.95
    1. Three Stooges films—Miscellanea.   2. Three Stooges (Comedy
team)—Miscellanea.   3. Motion picture actors and actresses—United
States—Biography.   4. Comedians—United States—Biography.
I. Title.
PN1995.9.T5S76   1988
791.43'028'0922—dc19   88-18877
                                                            CIP

Published by Contemporary Books, Inc.
180 North Michigan Avenue, Chicago, Illinois 60601
Manufactured in the United States of America
Library of Congress Catalog Card Number: 88-18877
International Standard Book Number: 0-8092-4613-9

Published simultaneously in Canada by Beaverbooks, Ltd.
195 Allstate Parkway, Valleywood Business Park
Markham, Ontario L3R 4T8 Canada

Contents

Chapter 1
Curly Qs

Twenty questions that'll make you scratch your head 'til ya turn bald. But remember, "Truth Is Stranger Than Fiction, Judgie-Wudgie!"

1. Soupy Sales told author Ron Smith about the time he was in the Navy during World War II, went to California on leave, and by a stroke of fortune saw Curly sitting in a car. He shouted, "Hey, Curly!" What did Curly do?
   a) He shouted, "Hay is for horses!"
   b) He ran away.
   c) He went "Nyuk nyuk nyuk!" and did a few bits.

2. How often did Curly clip his hair to keep it Stoogical?
   a) Every morning
   b) Once a week
   c) Every 28 days

3. In *An Ache in Every Stake*, Moe called Curly "Chucklehead," "Turniphead," "Grapehead," and "You Ignoramus." But off stage, what did Moe call Curly?
   a) Puddin' head
   b) Jeero
   c) Babe

4. Michael Jackson says: "Curly had a magic. He was God-gifted—a natural. I love everything about Curly." He also admits:
   a) "As a kid I shaved my head like Curly."
   b) "As a kid I imitated Curly all the time."
   c) "I had a big pie fight with Diana Ross after we watched my Stooges videotapes."

5. When Curly said, "So it shouldn't be a total loss . . ." what did he usually do?
   a) He took a drink.

1

b) He took a bath.

c) He gave money to charity.

6. According to Jack Kerouac, what did Curly do?
   a) "Throw pies at the human race."
   b) "Muckle and yukkle and squeal."
   c) "Ride fast into the void of Goslow."

7. In a 1938 newspaper interview with Curly, Larry, and Moe, Curly described his entry into the group: "I had beautiful wavy brown hair and a waxed mustache. When I went to see Ted Healy about a job as one of his Stooges, he said, 'What can ya do?' I said, 'I dunno.' He said, 'I know what ya can do. Ya can cut yer hair off.' So I had my hair cut off, almost to the bone. I was all skull." Larry then added:
   a) "Moe and I made him eat a dozen pies so he'd fatten up like a big Stoogeball."
   b) "Moe and I cut his waxed mustache off while he slept."
   c) "Moe and I beat him and kicked him to see if he could be durable enough for the act."

8. Curly liked to say he could "clear out a room" when he did this:
   a) Get on his side on the floor and revolve in a circle.
   b) Do an impression of Mussolini.
   c) Fart.

9. In an interview with the author, Moe's son-in-law Norman Maurer explained why Curly used to fall to the floor and do his crazy backward dancing:
   a) "He could not remember his lines."
   b) "He did it once on stage to kill a big sewer beetle on the floor and kept it in ever since."
   c) "He tried ducking out of a close-up the camera had of Moe. He flopped down, and trying to get out of the way, he looked comical. That was the start of it."

10. In *The Stooge Chronicles*, Shemp's widow explained why Curly died young:
    a) "Too much violence, too much fat"
    b) "Too much sex, too much drinking"
    c) "Too many pies thrown, too many pies eaten"

11. When Curly would come over to Moe's house, he was never without something. What was it?
    a) A gift cake
    b) A hat
    c) Shemp

12. Curly once used his three famous catchphrases within one minute. He shouted, "I'm a victim of soicumstance!" and "That's a coincidence!" and "Oh! A backbiter!" Why did he say all these things?
    a) He was in court during divorce proceedings.
    b) He was in Washington, D.C., in 1946 meeting the president, vice-president and secretary of state.
    c) He was in the midst of a clay fight.

13. In 1933 Curly made an obscure MGM film with two other stooges. What were their names?
    a) Burly and Surly
    b) Alphonse and Gaston
    c) George and Joe

14. According to the *Los Angeles Times*, when Curly was divorced from his wife in 1946, she charged that he used foul language, intimidated her by keeping mean dogs in the house, pinched her, and:
    a) "Put cigars in the sink."
    b) "Covered parts of my body with pie filling."
    c) "Shaved his head in bed."

15. In *Tassels in the Air*, Curly went berserk whenever he saw a tassel. This might have baffled Freud, but not Moe. As Moe explained it:
    a) "Aw, he's just subnormal."
    b) "When he was a baby someone tickled him with a pussy willow."
    c) "His mother had a beard."

16. In *Dizzy Detectives*, Curly didn't have a gun. What was his excuse?
    a) "Last week I blew my brains out, and I decided not to take a chance on something serious happening!"
    b) "The landlord's baby was crying so I gave it to the baby to play with."

c) "The real Stooges are all in the NRA."

17. Curly's recipe: "a gallon of gasoline, two tumblers of bicarbonate of soda, an ounce of iodine, a pinch of mustard." What was he making?
    a) A cocktail for Moe
    b) Soup for a family of fire eaters
    c) Liquid hair bleach

18. What did Curly want to be when he grew up?
    a) A catcher for the Brooklyn Dodgers
    b) A dancer
    c) An optometrist

19. On "Late Night with David Letterman," Moe's daughter Joan showed a home movie of how Curly acted in private life:
    a) Curly threw a pie right into the camera.
    b) Curly read a soliloquy from Eugene Field's poem "John Smith" and the lines "My heart felt like a sodden, soggy donut in my chest."
    c) Curly dropped his pants.

20. When Curly was terminally ill, where did he go?
    a) Los Arms Hospital
    b) Baldy View Sanitarium
    c) Larry Fine's house

Answers to Chapter 1

1. c) He nyuked and did bits. What a guy!
2. b) Once a week
3. c) Babe
4. b) "As a kid I imitated Curly all the time."
5. b) He took a bath.
6. b) "Muckle and yukkle and squeal"
7. b) "Moe and I cut his waxed mustache off while he slept."
8. c) Fart
9. a) "He could not remember his lines."
10. b) "Too much sex, too much drinking"
11. b) A hat
12. c) He was getting the worst of it in the *Pop Goes the Easel* clay fight.
13. c) George (Givot) and Joe (Callahan)
14. a) His most heinous crime: putting cigars in the sink
15. b) The pussy willow tassled him for life.
16. b) He gave it to the landlord's baby to play with.
17. c) Liquid hair bleach, which turned three women bald in *Cuckoo Cavaliers.*
18. b) A dancer
19. c) Curly dropped his pants.
20. b) Baldy View Sanitarium. He died there.

Chapter 2
Moe? Waddya Know?

Have enough brains to answer questions about the brains of the outfit? "I'll make it so simple even *you* can understand it."

1. The origin of Moe's "pudding bowl" haircut was simple. As a child he discovered its comic effect when:
   a) His mother cut his hair by putting a pudding bowl on his head.
   b) He cut his hair himself because it was long and girlish—and ended up with the pudding bowl look.
   c) Shemp played a practical joke on him by dumping chocolate pudding in his hair, forming a "pudding bowl" shape.

2. For nearly a year, Moe was blind. It happened in childhood. The problem was:
   a) Shemp poked him in the eyes.
   b) Shemp picked him up, dropped him, and this caused nose and eye damage.
   c) Moe was just a victim of circumstance—in his case, a disease called curlis ocularis.

3. What was Moe's real name?
   a) Emo Horowitz
   b) Harry Moses Horwitz
   c) Morton Horwitz

4. What year did Moe make his first film?
   a) 1909 for Vitaphone
   b) 1919 for MGM
   c) 1930 for 20th Century–Fox

5. One of Moe's first jobs in show business was with Ted Healy in 1912. What did they do?
   a) They wore women's swimsuits and falsies and were part of a "Diving Girls" troupe that did a high-diving act.

b) They were dressed as two halves of a giant pie that broke apart during a one-act play called *Cookie Land.*
c) They played the devil and a piece of cheese in the old Broadway play *Devil in the Cheese.*

6. Once, fed up with show business, Moe quit to open an "odd lot" store that sold fire-damaged and auction-lot merchandise. What made the most money for him?
   a) See-through lace undies that he sold as "Coozy Ventilators"
   b) Bottles of a failed chocolate–root beer soda pop that he sold as "Brighto"
   c) Limburger cheese, which he sold as "Chemical Warfare Rat Repellent"

7. Jack Kerouac described Moe like this:
   a) "A long-haired beatnik who really beat"
   b) "Mopish, mowbry, mope-mouthed, mealy, mad . . ."
   c) "A bigger wiseguy than James Dean"

8. Joe Besser met The Three Stooges in vaudeville, when Shemp was in the act. The boys were all married, so disciplinarian Moe made sure his pals didn't dally with the chorus girls. What did Joe say that Moe did if he saw a Stooge with a chorus girl?
   a) He grabbed them by the hair and pulled them away.
   b) He shouted, "Stooge! Atten-SHUN! To the rear, MARCH!"
   c) He held out his hand and said, "You're either gonna get a slap or the clap!"

9. In *The Daily Mirror* in 1938, an interviewer asked Moe what the boys' mission was. Moe said:
   a) "To be recognized as the supreme ambassadors of the Public School Code of Boorishness."
   b) "To someday have a pie named after us."
   c) "I hate your face. Why don't you pull your bottom lip over it and bite it all off?"

10. Moe Howard never liked to be called a slapstick comic. In a letter to Stephen E. Bowles he suggested a better term for himself and the boys. What was it?
    a) "Farcical comedians"

b) "Comedy violationists"
c) "Physical social satirists"

11. When schoolkids asked Moe's son Paul what his father did for a living, what did Paul generally tell them?
a) He was a meter reader for the gas company.
b) He was one of the Marx Brothers.
c) He worked for the "We Never Sleep Bakery."

12. One of Moe's favorite films was *You Nazty Spy,* where he got a chance to parody Hitler. He also delivered some sharply satiric lines. How does this one go? "We must throw off the yoke of monarchy and make our country . . .
a) safe from monogamy."
b) safe from thrown yolks."
c) safe for hypocrisy."

13. Moe wasn't crazy about Milton Berle. This was because once on stage together
a) Berle was in drag and kissed him.
b) Berle slapped him and cracked a tooth.
c) Berle parted his hair in the middle and said, "Don't I look like Shemp?"

14. When the Stooges were rediscovered in the 1980s, *People* magazine reported on "nyuk-nyukking numbskull" Curly and "frizzy-haired fish-eyed" Larry. How was Moe characterized?
a) "The Marquis de Sade of the moron set"
b) "The ringworm ringleader"
c) "The lint-fringed sourball"

15. How tall was Moe Howard?
a) 5'0"
b) 5'4"
c) 5'8"

16. What color eyes did Moe have?
a) Finger-colored
b) Brown
c) Blue

17. Once Moe had a nightmare. What was it?
    a) He dreamed that his two Stooges were Bud Abbott and Lou Costello.
    b) He dreamed he extinguished a burning chicken with a hose and woke up to discover he had wet the bed.
    c) He dreamed he was in a Stooge comedy and bit his wife on the nose.

18. At the start of World War II, Moe told a reporter about his plan for world peace:
    a) "Arm the soldiers with pies."
    b) "Make world leaders wear their hair like me, Larry, or Curly. They'll feel too stupid to cause trouble."
    c) "Nobody gets hurt till the shooting starts. Our army of stooges would guarantee everyone would get hurt in training."

19. Moe fractured his ankle and was knocked unconscious doing something. What was it?
    a) Kicking Curly and falling down
    b) Dancing on "American Bandstand"
    c) Wearing high heels

20. Moe once defended Stooge violence by pointing a finger elsewhere. "We're not as sadistic as _____."
    a) Don Rickles
    b) Westerns
    c) The average little kid

Answers to Chapter 2

1. b) He cut his own hair.
2. b) Shemp dropped Moe and hurt his nose, which through complications caused temporary nerve damage.
3. b) Harry Moses Horwitz
4. a) 1909 for Vitaphone. He made many film appearances when the motion-picture business was in New York.
5. a) They did some of the stunt diving too dangerous for the real female members of the women's diving team.
6. a) "Coozy Ventilators"
7. b) Mopish, etc.
8. a) He grabbed them by the hair and pulled them away.
9. a) To be recognized as ambassadors of boorishness
10. a) "Farcical comedians"
11. a) As Moe's daughter Joan explained on "Late Night with David Letterman," Paul said Moe was a meter reader.
12. c) Safe for hypocrisy.
13. b) Berle hit too hard.
14. a) Marquis de Sade of the moron set.
15. b) Moe was 5'4".
16. c) Blue
17. b) He dreamed about a burning chicken.
18. c) Moe believed soldiers should hurt each other in training. Larry agreed: "It's a world peace idea, but we can't get anybody to take it seriously."
19. c) He was wearing high heels for a drag sequence in a Stooges short.
20. b) Westerns. He told the *New York Herald Tribune*, "We're not as sadistic as Westerns . . . in Westerns, kids are likely not to understand or not to like it when somebody doesn't get up . . . kids don't mind seeing somebody get it over the head so long as they know that person will get right up." He added in another interview with the paper a year later: "With all the rough stuff we had, nobody ever died. We always survived all the violence. You take a look at your Westerns. You can count the dead at the end . . . and social groups and organizations don't say a word."

Chapter 3
Larry Lore

Here's a Fine how do ya do. Do ya know how he did it? It wasn't easy being the Stooge in the middle. It was a middle life crisis!

1. Why didn't Larry like to watch his old shorts?
   a) "The pockets need to be mended."
   b) "I lived it and I can still taste the pies."
   c) "I notice all the mistakes I made."

2. When Larry was two years old, his mother came home with a little brother (Morris "Moe" Feinberg). What did Larry say when he saw the new baby?
   a) "It looks like a victim of circumstance."
   b) "Yuck, he's ugly. Throw him out the window."
   c) "What idiot put that there?"

3. When Larry was a child, he earned money playing the violin in amateur contests and later by imitating
   a) John Barrymore
   b) A chicken
   c) Charlie Chaplin

4. Larry's first appearance with The Three Stooges was unintentional. Straight man Ted Healy saw Larry watching from the wings, got him on stage, and did what?
   a) He pelted him with eggs and threw him off stage.
   b) He said, "Folks, meet the newest Stooge! Watch for him tomorrow night on this stooge—er, stage."
   c) He shouted, "Here's a Fine how do ya do."

5. Larry's first appearance in comedy sketches was as a boy in a vaudeville "school days" routine, similar to the Marx Brothers' "Fun in Hi Skule" and other Gus Edwards–type shows. What was this touring vaudeville sketch called?
   a) "Jules White's School Days"

b) "Jules Black's School Days"

c) "Elementary, My Dear Wits-End"

6. The Three Stooges pretended to be everything from artists to doctors. But in one film, Larry played a part he knew well. He had been a professional as a teenager! Which profession did Larry excel in?

a) Exterminator (*Ants in the Pantry*)

b) Tailor (*Sing a Song of Six Pants*)

c) Riveter (*How High Is Up*)

7. How did Larry's weird hairstyle evolve?

a) He picked it after recalling how strange his rabbi looked with bushy hair and a tight skullcap.

b) He didn't have time to dry his wet hair and it ended up looking ridiculous.

c) He once appeared on stage in a winter sketch wearing gag earmuffs, and adapted the idea.

8. In *All the World's a Stooge*, the boys were refugees. Curly and Moe played little boys (Frankie and Johnny), but frizzy-haired Larry played a little girl. He used his wife's name. What was it?

a) Mae

b) Mabel

c) May-Bea

9. When Larry was on the road a lot, not making much money, he'd come home to Philadelphia by train. When his brother arrived to pick him up, what did Larry always ask for?

a) A kiss and a hug

b) A shot and a beer

c) Breyer's ice cream and a Tastykake

10. Larry chirped, "If ya have a knick-knack with a nick in it, we'll knock the nick out of the knick-knack." How could he do it?

a) He invented the "Ham-Fist Hammer" with Curly and Moe.

b) He was selling the miracle-fluid Brighto.

c) He was selling "Nichol's Lickety-Split Nick Kit."

11. Larry's real name was Feinberg, and he was born in Philadelphia. But where were his parents from?
    a) Russia
    b) Bavaria
    c) Trenton, New Jersey

12. Larry was once the butt of Stooge violence offscreen:
    a) Moe dropped a pie on his head from a rooftop.
    b) Shemp tried to stuff his head into a turkey.
    c) Curly pushed him off the Staten Island ferry.

13. According to Larry's brother, Morris, Larry was hired to join The Three Stooges for one major reason:
    a) Ted Healy wanted to hire a Stooge who wasn't a Howard brother—in case the brothers all left.
    b) Ted Healy saw a rival comic with two stooges and insisted on having one more than the competition.
    c) Ted Healy was drunk at the time and didn't realize he'd hired another Stooge.

14. Larry's screen wives used different terms of endearment than his real wife did. In *Dizzy Doctors* what did his wife call him?
    a) "Tuber-nosed potatohead"
    b) "Blank-minded wiener"
    c) "Weasel-faced porcupine"

15. How tall was Larry Fine?
    a) 5'2"
    b) 5'4"
    c) 5'6"

16. Director Edward Bernds used to say that Larry was "flaky" and contributed strange ideas to the Stooges' comedy. Most weren't used. Some evidently were. Try to figure out what Larry said when, in a Stooge short, he was asked, "Were you born in this country?"
    a) "Only my nose."
    b) "No. Milwaukee."
    c) "I didn't come out of any kinda tree!"

17. Larry had good reason to resent the blue bloods of high

society. Back in the 1920s, he and the boys entertained at a private party for society types. He was aghast when:
a) Several began to snort cocaine and make fun of his nose.
b) He was told not to mingle with the guests—but couldn't get out of the way when one vomited on him.
c) They all shut their eyes and said, "We're the lost generation—we can't see! We can't see!"

18. After Larry suffered a stroke, Moe considered replacing him so that he and Joe DeRita could continue rather than go into retirement. Who became the third Stooge?
a) Joe Besser
b) Warner Wolf
c) Emil Sitka

19. In an unpublished interview done during his stay at the Motion Picture County Hospital, Larry noted that this man "had a filthy mouth and a worse mind. And nobody seemed to like him . . . but he liked us." Who was he talking about?
a) Jerry Lewis, appearing on a telethon with the Stooges
b) Harry Cohn, president of Columbia Pictures
c) Adolf Hitler, who screened Stooge shorts in the 1930s

20. The "Larry Fine Archives" in New York is a cult of Larry devotees who have done more than contribute to the book *Larry, The Stooge in the Middle.* They've created Larry T-shirts, Larry leaflets, and periodically inundate the city with cryptic posters of Larry. What is the slogan of the Archives—which appears under the posters of Larry's face?
a) "Don't Be Caught in the Middle."
b) "Larry Me, Larry Me."
c) "I Have Seen the Future and It's Fine."

Answers to Chapter 3

1. c) "I notice all the mistakes I made."
2. b) He looked yucky, according to Moe Feinberg, who wrote the book *Larry, The Stooge in the Middle*.
3. c) Charlie Chaplin
4. a) Larry hadn't learned the act yet, but Healy didn't care. He brought Larry out and whispered, "Ask me for an egg," and when Larry did, he got pelted.
5. b) "Jules Black's School Days." Larry was with the show for many years. And later, of course, hooked up with director Jules White.
6. c) He was a riveter at the Hog Island shipyard.
7. b) Larry's brother, Morris, claimed that Larry arrived late at the theater and owner Jake Shubert roughly dried his hair into a frizz. Moe claimed that Larry was just sitting in the dressing room one day and his hair slowly dried that way, amazing him and Ted Healy.
8. b) His wife's name was Mabel Haney.
9. c) The sweets
10. b) Larry believed in Dr. Bright's Brighto.
11. a) Larry Fine's family name was originally Frienchicov. When the family came from Russia it became Feinberg. He was born October 5, 1902.
12. a) Moe couldn't resist dumping on him one day.
13. b) Moe Feinberg told the *Philadelphia Evening Bulletin*: "Phil Baker was in town [Chicago] with his stooges, Beatle and Bottle. This irked Healy, who said, "Nobody is bigger than Healy. If Baker has two stooges, I get three!"
14. c) "Weasel-faced porcupine"
15. b) According to his brother, "Larry never got to be more than five feet four inches tall. He wore elevator shoes."
16. b) "No. Milwaukee."
17. b) He was told not to mingle with the guests—but couldn't get out of the way when one vomited on him. Moe told the story on "The Mike Douglas Show."
18. c) Emil Sitka worked out some routines early in 1975, and the boys were set to film a cameo in a movie called *Blazing Mattresses*, but then Moe became ill. When he felt better Moe decided lecture tours would be a less strenuous form of show biz than Stooging.
19. b) Harry Cohn
20. c) "I Have Seen the Future and It's Fine."

Chapter 4
Vintage Shemp Pain

If you can answer all these questions you could be the Heavyweight Shempion of the World!

1. Once an ad ran in *Screw* magazine with a drawing of Shemp. What was the caption?
   a) "A Typical Date-less Screw Reader"
   b) "Subscribe, Mongoose."
   c) "Shemp Fever . . . Catch It!"

2. Shemp was the "original" Stooge, since he worked with straight man Ted Healy alone, almost like Lou Costello with Bud Abbott. Newspaper critic Bide Dudley reviewed their act in *A Night in Spain* and commented, "Shemp is what might be called a scream. And the best part of it is
   a) It isn't a false face he wears on stage."
   b) Whenever he screams Healy puts a fist in his mouth."
   c) He can do dog impressions just by standing there."

3. Shemp was able to do one thing better than his brothers Moe and Curly, though they all could do it.
   a) He was the best boxer.
   b) He was the best ukelele player.
   c) He was the best baker.

4. Drafted during World War I, Shemp did not serve for long. According to Moe, what was Shemp's problem?
   a) "He was a bed wetter."
   b) "His feet were size 12 and flat as a pancake."
   c) "He kept telling officers, 'I ain't takin' any orders from you!' and they agreed he was impossible."

5. Shemp used to take the bus or the train all the time because:
   a) He liked to display his prowess at sneaking on without paying.

b) He was afraid of riding in cars ever since he drove one through a barbershop window.

c) He liked to try out slapstick on the passengers and would suddenly squeal, "Eeb-eeb-eeb-eeb-eeb!"

6. Shemp and Moe went into vaudeville together in 1917, but before that they surprised friends by doing something else together. What did they do?
   a) They dated Siamese twins.
   b) Each grew a beard on only one side of his face.
   c) They dressed up as Woodrow Wilson and his wife and protested World War I on Nostrand Avenue.

7. Shemp left the Stooges before they signed with Columbia. He wanted to play a character in the *Joe Palooka* movie series. What was the character's name?
   a) Shemp
   b) I. M. Hoamly
   c) Knobby

8. In 1939 Shemp and a guy named Jack Edelstein opened a nightclub called *Stage One*. As *Variety* reported in March of that year:
   a) "It's the cat's meow. Plenty of hot patooties to look at and a yock a minute."
   b) "To the stone sober and discriminating it's no go . . . it looks like a losing struggle . . . there's table space for 300 but it's a waste of acreage."
   c) "That wise guy better get Larry and Moe to come spruce up the joint . . . put up wallpaper and maybe even do a comedy act to save the mortgage."

9. When Shemp made a film called *The Leather Pushers* with Andy Devine, he perfected a unique mannerism—a nervous lip twitch before he'd speak. He had a name for it:
   a) "The Ol' Twitcheroo"
   b) "The Ebee-Bebee"
   c) "The Fish-Mouth"

10. When Shemp and the boys were on stage, they used this joke. Moe: "Is that your right face?" Shemp:
    a) "It ain't anybody else's butt!"
    b) "No, it's my left face. It's a leftover!"
    c) "It was until somebody sat on it."

11. When The Stooges harmonized (either on the phone, or to tell somebody to "Come in . . . come in . . . come IN!!"), which voice was usually Shemp's?
    a) The lowest
    b) The highest
    c) The one in the middle

12. On live TV with Ed Wynn, Moe, Larry, and Shemp unveiled a new sadomasochistic comedy stunt, "The Double Zinger." Moe let Ed Wynn do the job:
    a) Wynn held out two fingers on each hand—and Larry and Shemp ran into them and poked their eyes.
    b) Wynn stuck a shish-kebab skewer through Larry and Shemp's ears.
    c) Wynn had Larry and Shemp drop ice cubes down the front and back of their pants.

13. On "The Mike Douglas Show" Moe recalled that Shemp always carried something in his pockets:
    a) Peanuts—in case he passed a park squirrel
    b) Rubbers—in case it began to rain
    c) Gag women's underwear—in case a panhandler asked him for "spare change"

14. Shemp once told a reporter that there was one thing about Stooge scripts that bothered him:
    a) "They don't exist."
    b) "I can't memorize them."
    c) "They're too formal. On top of my dialogue they always write, 'Samuel, Stooge #3.' "

15. Shemp had some pet names for things. What or who was "cackle fruit"?
    a) His wife, who always laughed in the audience
    b) His name for any effeminate stagehand
    c) Eggs

16. In *Pardon My Clutch*, Shemp was excited when he saw a doorknob. What did he think it was?
    a) The Pearl of Barrazaboo
    b) His bad tooth
    c) The onion that rolled away while he was cooking

17. In *Baby Sitters' Jitters* how did Shemp manage to calm a crying baby?
    a) He gave it a gun to suck on.
    b) He tickled it under the chin with a torn-out clump of Larry's hair.
    c) He stood on his head.

18. When Shemp had a good idea, what did he usually ask Larry and Moe to do?
    a) Grab his head and beat it out of him.
    b) "Pay me or I won't tell it to you."
    c) Draw him a hot bath so he could rest his tired brain.

19. Sometimes Shemp would walk down the street with a stick. What was the reason?
    a) It was for a gag. Someone was bound to ask him why and he'd answer, "I'm Divine. And this is my divining rod!"
    b) He was prepared to defend himself against threatening dogs.
    c) It was at a time when he wasn't married. He sported a sweater that said "Stick with Me, Kid" on the back.

20. When a reporter mentioned that Shemp was considered one of the ugliest men in Hollywood, what did he say?
    a) "I'm losing my teeth. I've got pyorrhea."
    b) "I'm a beast!"
    c) "I'm the best looker in my family."

Answers to Chapter 4

1. c) "Shemp Fever . . . Catch It!" Somebody over there liked Shemp.

2. a) "It isn't a false face he wears on stage."

3. b) He was the best ukelele player.

4. a) "He was a bed wetter."

5. b) He hated cars. Ironically, he dropped dead while riding in one.

6. b) They walked down the street wearing half a beard each.

7. c) Knobby (Knobby Walsh)

8. b) *Variety* said it was a no go, only "for those with a few on board and easy to please."

9. c) "The Fish-Mouth." As he explained to the *Morning Telegraph* on December 3, 1931: "Just before I started the first scene with Andy, I gave him the fish-mouth. He like to died. I had a nice speaking part, so what did they do? They had me be a fish-mouth all through the show. I wound up without a line." Shemp used the fish-mouth in many a Stooge short, too.

10. a) "It ain't anybody else's butt."

11. a) The lowest, as in *Baby Sitters' Jitters.*

12. a) Larry and Shemp had to willingly run into Wynn's outstretched fingers and gouge their eyes.

13. b) Rubbers. Shemp always worried about getting caught in the rain.

14. b) "I can't memorize them." He once explained that he would only look at the script for content, and then ad-lib stuff. He didn't follow it word for word. "I can't study a script," he said. "I inhale it."

15. c) Eggs. Sometimes he called them "hen fruit." In *Of Cash and Hash* he made "cackle soup"—by pouring hot water over a raw chicken.

16. b) The bad tooth he thought he'd extracted.

17. c) He stood on his head.

18. a) Beat his head. Usually the idea was in there but stuck. "I got it! I got it!" he'd shout at last. "What?" "A terrific headache . . ."

19. b) He was prepared to defend himself against threatening dogs.

20. b) "I'm a beast!"

Chapter 5

Besser Late Than Never

That craaaaazy was only a Stooge for a few years, but he sure was good in a pinch.

1. Joe's Orthodox Jewish parents called him "Jessel," which is the Hebrew version of Joseph. But what does "Besser" mean in Yiddish?
   a) Better
   b) A Tailor
   c) Pincher

2. Like The Three Stooges, Joe Besser had his problems when he played Great Britain. As a solo comic in the late 1930s he opened at the London Palladium and in the course of his act went "Woo woooo! I'm a cowwwwww boy!" The audience roared because:
   a) "Cow" meant "whore" in British slang.
   b) Tanaka Wu-Wu was a notorious opium den owner.
   c) "I'm a cowboy" was a catchphrase for "gay hustler" in Soho.

3. Joe's autobiography, published by Excelsior Books, was titled:
   a) *Ooooh, I'll Harm You!*
   b) *Besser Late Than Never*
   c) *Not Just a Stooge*

4. Strangely, Joe's teen years resembled Stooge comedies. Which *didn't* he do?
   a) Played with a boomerang—which boomed back into a window.
   b) Slid away so that the angry school principal spanked the chair instead of Joe's backside, then escaped by

crashing through a window.
c) Got in a tizzy during a family banquet and smashed his aunt in the face with an éclair.

5. Joe got into lots of mischief as a kid. So, once again, try to figure out which Stoogical thing this teen *didn't* do.
   a) He got the keys to a car, attempted to drive it forward but reversed it—crashing through a wall.
   b) He hopped onto a beer wagon and, like a "Beer Barrel Polecat," accidentally knocked barrels of beer into the street and made a foamy mess.
   c) He pinched his snoring father, shouting, "Not so LOUD!"

6. Many popular stars, such as Lucille Ball and Walter Brennan, got their start in Stooge comedies. Which 1960s TV star appeared in a Stooge short with Joe Besser?
   a) Bob Denver
   b) Dan Blocker
   c) Martin Milner

7. In *Quiz Whiz*, Joe decided to invest all his money in something. What was it?
   a) Consolidated Fuzz and Amalgamated Lint
   b) Consolidated Fujiyama California Smog Bags
   c) Consolidated Fat in the Can

8. In Joe's autobiography he mentioned a famous comedian who used to pal around with him. "My style and mannerisms undoubtedly influenced him," Joe wrote. "He incorporated some of the childlike inflections I did in his own character. Not intentionally, though." Who was he?
   a) Jerry Lewis
   b) Curly Howard
   c) Lou Costello

9. Joe's wife was a showgirl, and her initial reaction to him was similar to the reaction most women had toward the Stooges. Which of the following didn't she do before they got to know each other better.
   a) Sarcastically suggested he get out of show business and told everyone she never wanted to work with him.

b) Asked how much he would charge to haunt a house.

c) Threw his portable radio out the window and smashed it into the street.

10. Young stars appreciated Joe's years of experience in vaudeville and films. During the making of 1948's *Flying Squadron*, supporting actor Joe coached and advised a rising star who later insisted Joe was "the man who helped me believe in myself." Who was the actor?
    a) Paul Lynde
    b) Rock Hudson
    c) Ernest Borgnine

11. "I waited 21 years for this break," Joe Besser told a reporter for the *Morning Telegraph*. He was glad to get a chance to work with:
    a) The Three Stooges
    b) Abbott and Costello
    c) Olsen and Johnson

12. Joe Besser attracted plenty of attention in the 1940s. Who wrote this when Joe appeared on Broadway in 1942? "Out of the maelstrom of sound and fury there emerged on opening night a genial comedian who ran away with the show. . . . He is Joe Besser."
    a) Franklin Delano Roosevelt, in a letter
    b) Ed Sullivan, in a newspaper column
    c) John Barrymore, in a telegram to Lionel Barrymore

13. When Joe was a rising Broadway star, reporters came to interview him to find out more about his life. According to a piece in the January 12, 1942, issue of the *Toledo Blade*, what was Joe Besser's hobby?
    a) He "stands in front of a mirror and practices sissy boy gesticulations, considering it a form of play."
    b) He "builds Adirondack chairs and burns designs in wood."
    c) He "collects spoons which he paints into the likenesses of celebrities he's worked with."

14. How did Moe describe Joe Besser in one of the Stooge shorts?

a) "Two hundred and twenty pounds, five-foot-five by five-foot-five."
b) "Three hundred pounds of little kid—with a goat brain."
c) "Two hundred and fifty pounds. And 250 pounds of it is from the neck down."

15. Some fans have noticed that Moe didn't eye-poke or smack Besser the way he did Curly or Shemp. This was because:
a) Moe said he could only "let loose" with his brothers.
b) Joe's contract contained a clause prohibiting Moe and Larry from performing unnecessary acts of violence on him.
c) As part of the 1950s "Red Scare," a censor was constantly on the set to make sure un-American acts of aggression did not take place.

16. Though some saw the Besser shorts as sitcoms short on violence, in *Rusty Romeos* Larry's nose was scissored, Joe was hit with a flower pot, Moe inflated Larry's stomach with a bellows full of coal dust, and Larry hit Moe over the head with a shovel ten times. What was Joe's act of violence—to his girlfriend in the film?
a) He pinched her arm and said, "Oooh, you!"
b) He kissed her and she swooned.
c) He filled a rifle with tacks and shot them into her bottom—then spanked them in deeper with the barrel.

17. Many stars have teamed to star as comic crime-fighters. In the 1980s there have been such combos as Eddie Murphy and Judge Rheinhold, Bette Midler and Shelley Long, Billy Crystal and Gregory Hines. In 1950 Joe made a TV pilot pairing him as the detective partner to:
a) Hillary Brooke
b) Boris Karloff
c) Sheldon Leonard

18. Who were "Puttypuss," "Scare Bear" and "Cupid"?
a) Joe's pet cats
b) The nicknames given Moe, Joe, and Larry by Jules White during the making of the shorts
c) Characters Joe played when he worked doing voices for Saturday morning cartoons

19. When reporters asked Joe for his reaction to the hit tune "The Curly Shuffle," what did he say?
    a) "Is it a card game, like whist?"
    b) "That's nothin', some fans sent me a new song called "The Besser Mince," and it'll be a bigger hit, you crazy, you!"
    c) "The song really doesn't mean anything to me. It's nice for the boys, but I'm not Curly, I'm Joe Besser."

20. In a letter to author Ron Smith, Joe Besser wrote that in 1958 he left the Stooges and was replaced by Joe DeRita. He added:
    a) "The years with the boys were great, but, remember, I'm not just a stooge."
    b) "Ooooh, what a crazy! DeRita didn't look like me at all. I'm surprised they ever succeeded in features!"
    c) "I have been sorry ever since that I left the Stooges. We enjoyed working together and had a lot of fun."

Answers to Chapter 5

1. a) Better
2. a) In his autobiography he revealed that "cow" evidently meant "whore," and that the audience never heard the "boy."
3. c) *Not Just a Stooge*
4. c) He wasn't an éclair fighter.
5. c) No pinches
6. b) Dan Blocker, as a creature in *Outer Space Jitters*
7. b) Consolidated Fujiyama California Smog Bags
8. c) Lou Costello
9. b) She didn't use the "haunted house" line.
10. b) Rock Hudson
11. c) Olsen and Johnson. In 1942 Besser got his big break earning rave reviews supporting the duo in their "Sons o' Fun" review.
12. b) Ed Sullivan
13. b) He built Adirondack chairs "to while away spare time."
14. a) "Two hundred and twenty pounds, five-foot-five by five-foot-five." It was in *Quiz Whiz.* Moe added: "Color of hair? Skin!"
15. b) Joe's contract prohibited him from taking unnecessary abuse—and he determined what was necessary.
16. c) He shot his girlfriend in the butt for cheating on him with Moe and Larry—a heinous crime.
17. c) Sheldon Leonard
18. c) Cartoon characters
19. c) The song meant nothing to him.
20. c) "I have been sorry ever since that I left the Stooges. We enjoyed working together and had a lot of fun."

Chapter 6
DeRita's Digest

When the Stooges went into orbit and around the world in a daze, they did it 'cause they had DeRita stuff! Think you know Joe, buddy boy?

1. We all know the real names of Moe, Curly, Shemp, Larry and Joe Besser (don't we?). But what about Joe DeRita's real name?
   a) Joe DeRita
   b) Joe Wardell
   c) Joe DeMaestri

2. Throughout his teen years Curly Joe appeared in one play and played one part, touring the country's vaudeville circuit. He was:
   a) Cubby, The Chubby Cub Scout
   b) Peck's Bad Boy
   c) Peck's Buddy Boy

3. During World War II the ex-vaudevillian entertained the troops with a comedy act. Who was his straight man?
   a) Harry Langdon
   b) Harry Krishner
   c) Randolph Scott

4. What was Joe doing when he was offered the role of the third Stooge?
   a) He was out of work.
   b) He was working in Minsky's burlesque.
   c) He was getting a haircut.

5. Strangely, the first test gigs Curly Joe did with The Three Stooges were a flop. When the boys made their official "kiddie nightclub" debut, Curly Joe had changed. What had he done?

a) Gained 89 pounds.
b) Shaved his head.
c) Inserted cotton in his mouth so he'd talk funnier.

6. In 1959 Curly Joe and the boys made *Have Rocket Will Travel*. But they were mildly annoyed over two of the following three things. Which *wasn't* a problem?
a) Columbia tried to beat 'em to the punch with *Three Stooges Fun-O-Rama*, using old shorts with ex-Stooge Joe Besser.
b) Their comeback was merely part of a double bill—the co-feature was a Michael Landon movie based on a Kingston Trio song called "Tom Dooley."
c) Their comeback was merely part of a double bill—the co-feature was a James Garner movie based on a Ray Peterson song called "Tell Laura I Love Her."

7. It was with Curly Joe that the Stooges made their first "million-dollar movie" in 1961. In fact, it cost more than three million, the most for any Stooge flick. What film was it?
a) *The Three Stooges Meet Hercules*
b) *The Three Stooges Go Around the World in a Daze*
c) *Snow White and The Three Stooges*

8. Joe DeRita did make movies before he joined the Stooges. What part did he have in 1958's *The Bravados*?
a) The owner of a bakery
b) An extremely ugly woman
c) A hangman

9. Moe had some trouble with Curly Joe on stage, and it led to accidents. According to Moe, Curly Joe was:
a) "Leaning his face into my slaps, the gum-brain."
b) "Sweating so much around the head my hands slip when I'm supposed to catch him and his head hits the stage."
c) "Turning in the wrong direction during the eye pokes and making me slam my fingers against his skull."

10. One of Curly Joe's most memorable encounters with fans was in an elevator in Philadelphia. Two little girls rushed

in and did what?
a) Both had shaved their heads and told him it was so he'd see them in the audience during the show that night.
b) The girls hopped up on either side of him and kissed him on both cheeks, saying, "This is to make up for what that mean mongoose Moe always does."
c) One of them grabbed the cigar out of his mouth and the other uppercutted him on the chin.

11. Romantically, an unusual fact about Curly Joe is:
a) He got sexier as he got older—and was married in 1966 after giving a rootin' tootin' performance in *The Outlaws Is Coming*.
b) During his days with Minsky's burlesque, strippers once held a contest to see whose breasts were as large as his bald head.
c) In 1987 he received 389 marriage requests—from the entire female graduating class of Keim College, of Princeton, New Jersey.

12. Joe was actually the hero of *The Outlaws Is Coming*. What was his invention that saved the day?
a) Daylight saving time
b) A homing-pigeon arrow made of pigeon feathers that always landed on target—on a bent-over backside
c) "The All-Purpose Hunting Horn"

13. In *Snow White and The Three Stooges*, Curly Joe sold a magic elixir of youth. What was it called?
a) Magic Elixir of Youth
b) Buddy Boy's Beer
c) Yuk

14. Some Stooge fans consider the movies Curly Joe made with the Stooges as their weakest work. Reflecting on his 12 years as one of The Three Stooges, what was Curly Joe's opinion?
a) "The Stooges were darn funny, and if you think I took all that abuse for nothing, I'll shave your head and poke your eyes out."
b) "The Stooges were best with me because there was less violence. We were jolly old Santa Claus men who

treated the kiddies like our very own darling elves."
c) "I don't think the Stooges were funny. I'm not putting you on."

15. It's hard to find much on Joe DeRita's thoughts or attitudes toward his peers, but to Moe's daughter Joan he did express an opinion about someone: "He had a personality like the bottom of a birdcage." Who bore the distinction of being insulted by Joe DeRita?
a) Benito Mussolini
b) Jerry Lewis
c) Ed Sullivan

16. Joe, a consummate actor, sometimes voiced disdain for less skilled thespians. Who did he say was one of the worst actors in movies?
a) Joe Besser
b) George Raft
c) Sean Penn

17. In his autobiography, Moe recalled seeing Joe DeRita stark naked. Moe was amazed because:
a) DeRita had tattooed the words "Curly Joe" around his navel.
b) The bulgy body could've been a man's or a woman's.
c) Joe told him he regularly visited nudist colonies on his vacations.

18. Joe DeRita tried to revive The Three Stooges in 1974 (a year before Moe and Larry died). After a few concerts Joe's health forced the group to disband. Who were the other two Stooges?
a) Moe Howard and Larry Fine
b) Frank Mitchell and Mousie Garner
c) Moe Howard and Emil Sitka

19. What was the name of the TV pilot that Curly Joe and the boys made in 1969—after their movie days were over.
a) "Have Stooge Will Travel"
b) "Gunther Less and the Morons"
c) "Kook's Tour"

20. *The Outlaws Is Coming* was the last Three Stooges film. What was Curly Joe's prophetic last line in the film?
    a) "In another 20 years I'll be 79 and the last Stooge."
    b) "Hey Moe! Hey Larry! Aw, come on, the fun's not over yet, is it?"
    c) "Just like in the big-budget Westerns—we're gonna get to ride off into the sunset . . ."

Answers to Chapter 6

1. b) Joe Wardell
2. b) Peck's Bad Boy
3. c) Randolph Scott
4. b) He was working for Minsky.
5. b) He shaved his head. He'd worn longer hair, and then a full crewcut. The less pressure on the brain the better!
6. c) Their comeback was not part of a James Garner flick called *Tell Laura I Love Her*. That film was never made—or even contemplated.
7. c) *Snow White and The Three Stooges*
8. c) A hangman
9. b) Joe was sweaty!
10. c) The girls gave him a double dose of slapstick, as Joe sadly related in a *New York Times* interview on June 26, 1958.
11. a) He got married.
12. c) "The All-Purpose Hunting Horn." It could lure ducks, or even a herd of buffalo.
13. c) Yuk
14. c) Curly Joe, as a student of comedy, felt that the Stooges were too obvious. Other comics created "accidental" slapstick that looked spontaneous. "Laurel and Hardy . . . I can watch their films [over and over] . . . but when I see that pie or seltzer bottle, I know that it's not just lying around for no reason."
15. c) Ed Sullivan
16. b) George Raft
17. b) The hanging flesh made him look androgynous.
18. b) Frank Mitchell and Mousie "They Wanted Me for the Third Stooge All the Time, Really They Did" Garner
19. c) "Kook's Tour"
20. c) "Just like in the big-budget Westerns—we're gonna get to ride off into the sunset . . ."

Chapter 7
Photo Quiz I

1. True or False: The Stooges were a ribald vaudeville act and once broke into song with "I took my girl to Miami, and now I'm going to Tampa with her!"

2. Stooges and guns don't go together. Which Stooge accidentally shot himself in the foot in real life?

3. Moe and author Ron Smith began their correspondence back in the mid-1960s. In one letter Moe noted that "We wrote about 80 percent of every comedy we made mostly because most writers . . ."
   a) were appleheads."
   b) didn't understand our type of comedy."
   c) worked so cheap at Columbia they couldn't afford enough paper to complete a script."

4. According to Curly's wife, Elaine, "He was a cutup when we were out in public." He liked to bend spoons and play them, and he also
   a) did the "oyster in the soup" routine.
   b) ripped tablecloths in time to the music.
   c) pretended to shave his bald head with a butter knife.

5. We know Larry was a fine violinist as a kid. But at 14 Larry was also a pro boxer. What name did he use?
   a) Kayo Stradivarius
   b) Larry "Illegal Parking" Fine
   c) Kid Roth

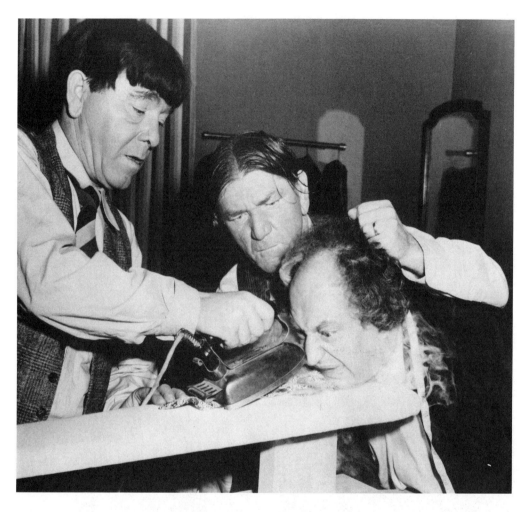

6. Moe dishes out the violence. Larry's steamed! In the *New York Herald Tribune*, in June 1961, he defended Stooge violence and said members of only one group seemed to find fault: "Women who are frustrated at home and don't dare talk to their husbands or they'll get a smack in the kisser object to the violence in our shows." He figured these women were
   a) "isolated members of the PTA."
   b) "ladies so frozen you'd think they sat on a big cake of ice all day."
   c) "members of the Communist Party."

7. Curly could come up with some pretty strange faces. Fans
   who looked closely could see one mark, a scar high on his
   cheek. What caused it?
   a) Moe threw an egg beater at him in *Three Smart Saps*.
   b) Larry sprayed him with seltzer, and a glass chip from
      the bottom of the bottle hit Curly in the face.
   c) Curly got himself into a car accident.

8. After the original Stooges left Ted Healy, he got new ones. This trio billed themselves as "Ted Healy's Original Three Stooges" until the *real* originals sued 'em! Then they became "The Gentlemaniacs." In 1986 they reunited as The Three Stooges for club dates. Over the years, five guys were in the troupe: Mr. Wolf, Mr. Wolfe, Mr. Garner, Mr. Mitchell, and Mr. Hakins. Get at least three of their first names right!

9. Some thought the Stooges vocalizing was worse than nails scraping on a blackboard. Here's a toughie. When the original Three Stooges harmonized (to sing "Hello, Hello, Hello," or hawk fresh "Catfish, Catfish, Catfish," etc.), who had the low voice, who had the high voice, and who sang in the middle register?

10. "Don't just sit there—get up and dance!" The boys inspired "The Curly Shuffle," and a funky disco version of "The Alphabet Song" recorded by Malcolm McLaren for his 1986 "Swamp Thing" album. What did he call his dance version of "The Alphabet Song?"
    a) "The Alphabet Song"
    b) "Get Up, Get Down, Pick Two"
    c) "B-I-Bicki"

Answers to Chapter 7

1. True. The next line: "Well, if you don't, Jacksonville." Mild stuff, but a review in *Variety* in January 1938 claimed that "some of their material is pretty much on the blue side." And according to *Variety* in August 1938, "Some of their wisecracks are a little shady." In April 1940, *Variety* was still griping that the boys "allow vulgarity to creep in."

2. Curly. He shot himself in the foot. He was 13. Strangely, in *Dizzy Detectives* there was a scene where he shot himself in the toe. To which Moe said, "Next time you handle a gun shoot yourself in the head!"

3. b) Didn't understand our type of comedy."

4. b) He ripped tablecloths in time to the music.

5. c) Kid Roth. He had one fight, won it, and retired.

6. a) "Isolated members of the PTA" (Parent/Teachers Association)

7. c) Curly was involved in a car accident when he was 20.

8. They were Jack Wolf, Sammy Wolfe, Mousie Garner, Frank Mitchell, and Dick Hakins. Mousie, as he's often said, once auditioned for Moe and nearly became a legit "third Stooge."

9. In most films, including *Booby Dupes* and *Gents Without Cents*, Curly sang the low part, Moe the middle, and finally Larry came in as a tenor.

10. c) "B-I-Bicki"

Chapter 8
U. Syawitz

Ya gotta use your wits on this one. Try to figure out the gag name and where it belongs!

1. Costa Plente
2. Link, Pink, and Mink
3. Coffin Nail
4. Crumbette
5. Anna Sinnic
6. Anna Conda
7. Ziller, Zeller, and Zoller
8. Stincoala
9. Mishigoss
10. Captain Gorgonzola

a) A cigarette company
b) A hospital patient
c) A ritzy hotel
d) A surgical instrument
e) Larry in drag
f) Sausage makers
g) Psychiatrists
h) Ingredient in Shemp's "Fountain of Youth" formula
i) A leader in the Foreign Legion
j) A city in Moronica

Answers to Chapter 8

1. c) They stayed at this ritzy hotel in *Healthy, Wealthy and Dumb*.
2. f) Sausage makers in *If a Body Meets a Body*
3. a) The cigarette company at 1010 Tobacco Road, Virginia, Texas
4. e) Curly introduced Larry as Crumbette in *Pop Goes the Easel*.
5. d) A surgical instrument from *Men in Black*
6. b) A hospital patient
7. g) Psychiatrists the boys impersonated in *Three Sappy People*
8. j) Where the Wrong Brothers lived
9. h) It was in *All Gummed Up*.
10. i) He was captured in *Wee Wee Monsieur*.

Chapter 9
Funny Boy!

The boys didn't rely on sight gags alone. They put jokes into the scripts. They were dutiful—but dumb! Don't look blank, fill in the blanks and laugh again at those punch-drunk punch lines!

1. "These men can't be held for vagrancy," says a judge. "They have visible means of support."
   Larry: "Does he mean our _____?"

2. In *Busy Buddies* Curly is a crackpot cook. When he destroys a meal, a customer complains, but Curly has a rejoinder.
   Curly: "Are you casting _____ on my cooking?"

3. In *Dutiful but Dumb* the boys worked for "Whack Magazine." Their slogan was "If it's a good picture, it's ___ ___ _____."

4. Curly concocted a terrible pun in *Uncivil Warriors*. He tells an admiring cutie, "I used to work in a bakery as a pilot . . . Yeah, I used to take the bread from one corner and _____ __ ___ __ _____."

5. This was Moe's standard line when any Stooge snored in bed, used in *If a Body Meets a Body*, among others: "Hey, wake up and ____ ____ _____!"

6. Curly sang it: "She was bred in Old Kentucky, but she's only a _____ __ _____."

7. Curly: "What's that monkey got that I ain't got?"
   Moe: "A longer _____."

8. Curly: "If at first you don't succeed, _____ ____ _____ 'til you do succeed!"

9. In *Dancing Lady,* Moe said: "I'm the best musician in the country."
   Curly: "Yeah, but how are you __ ___ _____?"

10. The boys pretended to be reporters in *Three Little Beers.* That way they could sneak into a golf tournament with fake press passes.
    Moe: "Press."
    Larry: "Press."
    Curly: "_____."

11. "Did you take a bath?"
    "Why? Is _____ ___ _____?"

12. A yock from *Calling All Curs:*
    Curly: "I can't see! I can't see!"
    Moe: "Why not?"
    Curly: "I ___ ___ _____ _____!"

13. The boys are looking at antiques in a fancy hotel suite.
    Hotel manager: "This bed goes back to Henry the Eighth."
    Curly: "That's nothin', we had a bed that went back to _____ _____ __ _____."

14. In *An Ache in Every Stake,* Curly shaves a cake of ice, acting as if it's a customer in his barbershop.
    Curly: "Are you married or _____?"

15. Curly loved to sing 'em, but sometimes he barely got out the title of a tune before he got slugged. In a brief scene in *Booby Dupes* he offers this one.
    Curly: "Don't Chop the Wood, Mother, Father's Coming Home with __ _____."

16. In *Men in Black* the head of the hospital asks, "What do you men know about medicine?"
    Larry: "We graduated with the highest _____ in our class."

17. In *Dizzy Pilots* the boys are experts at building a plane. But they need the right equipment.
    Moe: "Where's the vise?"
    Curly: "Vice? I have no vice, I'm as pure as the driven snow!"
    Moe: "But you _____!"

18. Larry used this one quite a few times. Evidently it was his favorite gag. In *Uncivil Warriors* it went like this:
    Larry: "Excuse me, gentlemen, I've got to take care of a weak back."
    Straight man: "Pardon me. How long have you had a weak back?"
    Larry: "Oh, about __ _____ _____."

19. The boys dressed up as Scotsmen for *Pardon My Scotch*. A curious man from Scotland isn't sure he buys this.
    Scotsman: "Are you laddies from Loch Lomond?"
    Curly: "No! We're from Loch _____!"

20. *In the Sweet Pie and Pie* saw the boys in prison, mistaken for the "Mushroom Murder Mob." Fortunately, Curly has a saw.
    Moe: "Is this a musical saw?"
    Curly: "Why certainly! It plays 'I Hear a _____.'"

Answers to Chapter 9

1. "Does he mean our Suspenders?" Larry asked in *Listen Judge*, among other films.

2. "Are you casting asparagus on my cooking?"

3. "If it's a good picture, it's out of whack."

4. "I used to take the bread from one corner, and pile it in the other."

5. "Hey, wake up and go to sleep!"

6. "She was bred in Old Kentucky, but she's only a crumb up here."

7. "A longer tail."

8. "If at first you don't succeed, keep on sucking 'til you do succeed!"

9. "Yeah, but how are you in the city?"

10. "Pull!"

11. "Why? Is there one missing?"

12. "I got my eyes closed!"

13. "We had a bed that went back to Sears Roebuck the Third!"

14. "Are you married or happy?"

15. "Don't Chop the Wood, Mother, Father's Coming Home with a Load."

16. "We graduated with the highest temperatures in our class."

17. "But you drifted!"

18. "Oh, about a week back."

19. "No, we're from Loch Jaw!"

20. "I Hear a Ripsody."

Chapter 10
Three Sappy People

The Stooges are almost indescribable, but everyone's tried to describe 'em anyway. Below are some descriptions doled out by the press. Match them to the correct Stooge.

1. In 1938, the *Daily Mirror* said his most distinguishing feature was the "cuspidor bob."

2. In 1983, *Film Comment* described this Stooge as "sliding from Moe-aggressive to passed-out passive."

3. A February 1986 edition of the *Chicago Tribune* thought this word described him best: "Squeaky."

4. In March of 1983, the *New York Times* figured this Stooge's oddest facial characteristic was being "goggle-eyed."

5. The *Toledo Blade* decided that it wasn't Curly but this guy who could be a "moon-faced, merry-eyed, chubby little man."

6. According to an Associated Press story in 1961, this guy was just a "punching bag."

7. In the same story this Stooge was noted for "the querulous look."

8. In 1975, *Newsweek* called him "gimlet eye."

9. *TV Guide* in 1959 said his hair was "similar to what you'd find on a dirty tennis ball."

10. *TV Guide* also figured that this Stooge could be described as the one "of the butch haircut."

11. "Short, chubby, pink-faced with wide blue eyes from ear to ear" was one description of him in the *Morning Telegraph.*

12. Back in February of 1959, the *New York Post* rhapsodized about him as "a wild caricature of Leopold Stokowski."

13. In November 1971, *Applause* described him as having a "head like a hastily eaten bowl of spaghetti."

14. Thinking mathematically, *Applause* described this Stooge as being "shaped like a figure 8 with an abnormally small top loop."

15. The *New York Herald Tribune,* in June of 1961 thought it was simple. He was the "wild-haire l one who looks like a koala bear."

16. In 1982, the *Wall Street Journal* recalled that his main traits were being "chubby, squeally-voiced."

17. In February of 1959, the *New York Post* characterized his head as looking like a "half-shelled coconut."

18. In the *Morning Telegraph* he was analyzed in depth: "He had developed his own brand of swish and sway . . . done with a flick of the wrist, a twist of the hip, and a not-too-high falsetto."

19. Author Ron Smith writing in an issue of *Video* magazine: "His eyes were small and squinty, like raisins in thickened oatmeal. His nose was lumpy like an old potato. Greasy hair skittered down either side of his head from the part in the middle. His ears were the size of zwieback crackers. And his voice drifted between gruff wise guy and whining Stooge."

20. The *New York Times* in January of 1975 eulogized his "Aztec profile" and "hay-colored hair," two descriptions they found in a 1938 *New York Post* piece.

Answers to Chapter 10

1. Moe
2. Larry
3. Larry
4. Larry
5. Joe Besser
6. Curly Joe
7. Larry
8. Moe
9. Curly Joe
10. Curly Joe, again.
11. Joe Besser
12. Larry
13. Larry
14. Curly
15. Larry
16. Curly
17. Moe
18. Joe Besser
19. Shemp
20. Larry

Chapter 11

Do You Promise to Tell the Truth, the Whole Truth, and Nothing but the Truth?

Waddya got to lose? If ya get 'em wrong, just file Chapter 11 for bankruptcy! Nyuk, nyuk, nyuk.

True or False

1. Moe once defended the Stooge style of comedy by saying, "We do stupid things, but they're excusable because we don't know any better."

2. Comedian Harold Lloyd sued The Three Stooges for gag theft and won his case.

3. Christine McIntyre was actually a great singer and it was her voice that was used during the operatic "Voice of Spring" in *Micro-Phonies.*

4. The building called "Los Arms Hospital" in *Men in Black* is now the "Church of Scientology."

5. In addition to the Howard brothers—Moe, Curly, and Shemp— there were two Howard sisters, Jacqueline and Ida.

6. Everybody knows that Lucille Ball, Walter Brennan, and Lloyd Bridges appeared in Stooge films. But so did TV's

"Batman" (Adam West), "The Cisco Kid" (Duncan Renaldo), and "Tarzan" (Jock Mahoney).

7. TV's "Perry White" (John Hamilton), "Lois Lane" (Noel Neill), and radio's "Lone Ranger" (Brace Beemer) all worked in Stooge films.

8. Everyone's heard of Jerry Lester. That's actually Curly's real first and middle name.

9. The boys were once hired for "Three Musketeers" chocolate-bar ads, but their campaign was never used because an indignant executor of the Dumas estate objected to them.

10. Larry said that when he joined The Three Stooges he told Ted Healy, "I'm not nervous, I'm stupid."

11. Curly Howard never wore long hair in a film with The Three Stooges.

12. The Stooges made several color shorts for MGM, but nobody kept copies and they're all lost.

13. Ted Healy's Stooges were once "Moe, Shemp, and Ken."

14. In the finale cream-puff battle in *Half-Wits' Holiday*, two of the extras who were hit with pies were the then mayors of Los Angeles and San Francisco, both Stooge fans and thrilled to be hit by Moe in a film.

15. On "Late Night," David Letterman held up a can of Campbell's Curly Noodle Soup and said, "Personally, my favorite is the Shemp Broth."

16. "The Curly Shuffle" was a big hit record—it sold a quarter of a million copies in three weeks.

17. The same year that censors clipped violence from *King Kong*, Columbia censored a gag scene from *Uncivil Warriors* in which Moe pokes Curly in the eye, causing his eyeball to fly out and snap back. Private collectors have it, but Columbia refuses to restore it to the original print.

18. Moe Howard and Albert Einstein appeared in an ad campaign together.

19. Though he was told to control his "killer instincts" in *Disorder in the Court,* Moe actually saved lives when he worked as a lifeguard in real life.

20. Larry's morning ritual before each day's shooting was to wet his head in a basin of beer to make it suitably frizzy.

Answers to Chapter 11

1. True. He said it in a 1959 interview with the *New York Herald Tribune*.

2. True. In *Loco Boy Makes Good* writer Clyde Bruckman used material he'd already given to Harold Lloyd for a silent movie many years earlier. The Stooges, of course, were completely innocent—victims of soicumstance.

3. True

4. True

5. False. There were two other brothers, Jack and Irving.

6. True. Jock Mahoney made several Stooge shorts with Shemp, Adam West was in *The Outlaws Is Coming* and Duncan Renaldo played a villain in *I'll Never Heil Again*.

7. False. Only one of them did—John Hamilton. He appeared in *Listen Judge*, on the receiving end of an exploding cake.

8. True. He could hardly be confused with the Jerry Lester who hosted the first "Tonight Show," which was actually called "Broadway Open House." Jerome Lester Horwitz was born October 22, 1903.

9. False

10. True

11. False. In *Goofs and Saddles*, for example, he played Buffalo Billious, and sported shoulder-length hair for a good portion of the film.

12. False. UA Classics put the shorts together for a 95-minute compilation movie, *The MGM Three Stooges Festival*, which was released in 1983. Only one short in the series, *Hello Pop*, has evidently been lost forever.

13. True. According to *Variety's* obituary of Kenneth Lackey (April 1976), "He worked briefly with Ted Healy in vaudeville and then teamed with Moe and Shemp Horowitz [sic] in 1923 to form the original Stooge act." He later retired to become a clerk in a U.S. District Court in Indiana.

14. False. And there was no cream-puff fight in *Half Wits' Holiday*—it was a pie fight.

15. True. Paul Schaffer was probably holding out for Joe Besser's Cream of Wienie.

16. True, according to the *Los Angeles Times*. Fifty thousand copies were sold in Chicago before it was bought by Atlantic and issued nationally.

17. False. The Stooges weren't even making films for

Columbia the year *King Kong* was released.

18. True. But neither of them was alive to see it. In 1987 Nikon ran side-by-side pictures of Moe and Einstein with cameras superimposed around their necks. The pitch was: "You don't have to be a genius to use the new Nikon N4004."

19. True. Moe was a fine lifeguard in his early years in Brooklyn.

20. False

Chapter 12
Be a Stooge!

What would Emily Post say? In this chapter you get your fondest wish: to actually star as one of The Three Stooges. Now mind your Ps and Qs, and see if you know how to act like a real Stooge!

1. When you're asked to make "canapes," what do you do?

2. Moe's just yelled "Gimme a hand!" What's the correct stupid Stooge reply?

3. You're at a banquet table and you're slurping your coffee from the saucer while holding it with both hands. When Moe says, "Ain't ya got no etiquette," you should do something. What?

4. You're a scientist with half a brain, mixing up chemicals to invent a new wonder tonic. But, Stooge, you don't use a mixing bowl, a test tube, or a jar. Soitanly not. Waddya use?

5. You take out a cigar, but before you smoke it, you gently put it to your ear for a minute. Why?

6. You have a bad cold and a stuffy nose. Moe helps by handing you a small jar of salve. Naturally you aren't paying attention and, naturally, there's another jar within your grasp. What's in the other jar?

7. You and Larry have just finished painting the stairs. Now Larry wants to get downstairs without leaving his footprints on the stairs. What's your Stooge solution?

8. Now it's time to help Curly. You're at work on a skyscraper beam high above the city. Curly tells you he's afraid of heights. What do you do to help him work?

9. You tried to walk through a doorway, but one of the Stooges flanked you. Now you're both wedged in the doorway. What do you say?

10. There is a specific reason why you would kiss a woman's hand. What is it?

Answers to Chapter 12

1. You make canapes by putting canned peas on dog biscuits. If you just said, "Grab a can a' peas," you get it half right, halfwit!
2. "Which one?"
3. Continue drinking from the saucer—but raise your pinkies!
4. A big rubber boot.
5. To listen to the band!
6. Limburger cheese, which you smear all over yourself. As the dialogue went in *All The World's a Stooge*: "Since I got this cold, I don't smell so good." "I'll say you don't!"
7. Carry him downstairs. (See *Tassels in the Air*.)
8. Blindfold him. That was the solution in *How High Is Up*.
9. "Recede!"
10. To bite the diamond off her ring. Curly did it in *Half-Wits' Holiday*.

Chapter 13
Ann Uther

Oh, superstitious, eh? Why is it everyone the Stooges meet has a name that means something? Why is it that every place was named by a wise guy? Match the numbers to the letters.

1. Tinctura Nucis Vomige
2. Tsimmis
3. Cut Throat
4. Hangemall
5. Ba Loni Sulami
6. I. Yankum
7. Hart, Burns & Belcher
8. Fuller Bull
9. Gypsom Good
10. Gin Rickia and Mikey Finlen

a) A prison
b) A dentist
c) Label on a drug bottle in a pharmacy
d) Though a Jewish word, it was an Arab desert city.
e) A drug store
f) A medicine man and love-potion salesman
g) A sign on a door in a medical building
h) An antique dealer
i) Managing editor of "The Daily News"
j) Places on a map of South Starvania

Answers to Chapter 13

1. c) It was seen, but fortunately not used, in *Pardon My Scotch*.

2. d) You can find the city in *Wee Wee Monsieur*. Tsimmis is a kind of stew with varying ingredients. No doubt the Howard brothers, Larry Fine, and Joe Besser remembered it from Sabbath meals in their childhood. The *Jewish Festival Cookbook* notes two variations: a tsimmis with carrots, sweet potatoes, and apples baked together, and another combining brisket, rutabaga, and onions—with a dash of nutmeg.

3. e) The Cut Throat Drug Store—where Shemp invented his "Fountain of Youth" potion.

4. a) A prison in which the boys, mistaken for the "Mushroom Murder Mob," were to be hanged.

5. f) Dr. Ba Loni Sulami appeared in *Three Missing Links*.

6. b) The boys used Dr. I. Yankum's office in *All the World's a Stooge*.

7. g) Drs. Hart, Burns & Belcher were out the night the three Stoogical janitors got into *A Gem of a Jam*.

8. i) Fuller Bull hired what he thought were reporters from "The Star Press" in *Crash Goes the Hash*.

9. h) It was in the offices of Gypsom Good that the boys discovered the escaped gorilla in *Dizzy Detectives*.

10. j) You could find those drinking terms (along with Hang Gover and Asperin) on a map in *You Nazty Spy*.

Chapter 14
The Date Quiz

Some of you well-informed imbeciles out there think you graduated from Watsammattawit U. This quiz isn't for everybody, just those die-hard Stoogephiles who have it *all* memorized. Or so they think. Simply match the date to the corresponding Stooge event.

1. 1922
2. 1925
3. 1932
4. 1934
5. 1946
6. 1952
7. 1955
8. 1958
9. 1959
10. 1975

a) The boys make their first feature with Joe DeRita.
b) The boys make their first short for Columbia.
c) Curly suffers a stroke.
d) Moe and Shemp join Ted Healy.
e) Shemp dies.
f) Larry joins the act, creating "The Three Stooges" for Ted Healy.
g) Moe and Larry die.
h) Curly dies.
i) Shemp leaves to go solo.
j) Joe Besser leaves the group when Columbia closes the shorts department.

Answers to Chapter 14

1. d
2. f
3. i
4. b
5. c
6. h
7. e
8. j
9. a
10. g

Chapter 15
Stooge Professions

The Stooges never held jobs for too long. See if you can remember these soicumstances.

1. In *How High Is Up* they owned "Minute Menders Inc." They charged "a nickel a hole." What did they do?
   a) They were gynecologists.
   b) They sewed underwear, shirts, and pants.
   c) They fixed punctured lunch boxes.

2. Curly was an inventor in *Cactus Makes Perfect*. What was his trickling brainstorm?
   a) Cactus toupees for aggressive people
   b) A retriever of gold-color buttons
   c) An egg separator

3. When the boys were out selling "Brighto," what was their slogan?
   a) "Every man for himself."
   b) "Sick 'em."
   c) "Makes old bodies new."

4. The boys were operating out of a truck marked "Star Cleaning Pressing Co." When the doors swung open and the sign changed, they were mistaken for:
   a) Astronomers
   b) Newspapermen
   c) "Staring" detectives

5. "We forgot to allow for shrinkage!" says Moe. What business were he and the boys in?
   a) They were psychiatrists.
   b) They worked in a laundry.
   c) They were icemen.

6. In *Hoi Polloi,* the boys are going to be made into "gentlemen." What were they before they joined "society"?
   a) Photographers
   b) Garbagemen
   c) Sewer workers

7. Larry said, "Oh! Oh! I got four kinks in my back!" What were the Stooges doing?
   a) They were doctors.
   b) They were owners of a pet shop.
   c) They were card players.

8. In *Some More of Somoa,* the boys called themselves "The Biggest Grafters in Town." What were they?
   a) Politicians
   b) Tree surgeons
   c) Graph paper salesmen

9. Curly insisted every man was a "potent hunter." That's why he and his pals became salesmen for a firm called:
   a) Ace Marriage Bureau
   b) Slip On a Banana Republic Tours
   c) Canvas Back Duck Club

10. Remember when they worked for the "King Winter Outfitting Company of Ticonderoga, New York"? If ya don't, go watch *Saved by the Belle* over again. Or take a guess: what were they actually selling?
    a) Live cats that people thought were fur hats
    b) Pillows to wear as earthquake shock absorbers
    c) Mustard plasters that could be wrapped around hot dogs

Answers to Chapter 15

1. c) Of course, they punctured 'em to drum up business!

2. b) A retriever of gold-color buttons

3. c) "Makes old bodies new." Dr. Bright's slogan, printed on their sample cases, was "Brightens old bodies." Not that the *Dizzy Doctors* cared.

4. b) Newspapermen. Vernon Dent thought they were with "The Star Press."

5. c) They were icemen, in *An Ache in Every Stake*.

6. b) Garbagemen

7. c) Card players, trying to cheat in *Goofs and Saddles*

8. b) They owned "Elite Painless Tree Surgeons."

9. c) Canvas Back Duck Club, for "potential," "potentate," and "potent" hunters

10. b) Pillows that could be strapped around the waist and used as shock absorbers. Their wardrobe idea was a hit 'til they ran afoul of dictator Ward Robey.

Chapter 16
I'll Annihilate Ya

Moe was one of the few guys who could make discipline funny. One of his trademarks was the use of venomous but inane threats. See if you can put these together.

1. From *Three Sappy People*:
   "Why don't you get a _____ with some brains in it!"

2. From *Spook Louder*:
   "I'll knock your head right through your _____!"

3. From *If a Body Meets a Body*:
   "I'll tear your _____ out and tie it around your neck for a bowtie!"

4. From *Booty and the Beast*:
   "I'll push that _____ right through the back of your head!"

5. From *Rusty Romeos*:
   "If I had a machine gun, I'd blow you to ribbons, you _____ head!"

6. From *Idle Roomers*:
   "I always said your _____ scares people. Why don't you throw it away?"

7. From *He Cooked His Goose*:
   "I'll tear that cucumber of yours off and shove it down your _____!"

8. From *Listen Judge*:
   "I'm gonna _____ you in nitric acid!"

9. From *Crash Goes the Hash*:
   "I'll tear your _____ out and shove it right in your eye!"

10. From *Three Sappy People*:
    "Remind me to tear out your _____!"

Choices (Fill in the blanks with these—but watch it, some are red herrings.)

a) eye
b) esophagus
c) throat
d) toupee
e) Adam's apple
f) red herrings
g) socks

h) tonsils
i) murder
j) baste
k) nuts
l) sponge
m) face
n) rhesus monkey

Answers to Chapter 16

1. d) toupee
2. g) socks
3. h) tonsils
4. a) eye
5. l) sponge
6. m) face
7. c) throat
8. j) baste
9. b) esophagus
10. e) Adam's apple

Chapter 17
Oh, Another Elwood Ullman!

The writers who worked with the Stooges were never given much credit. Yet the jokes they wrote were as important in establishing the Stooges' personality as the slapstick. So it shouldn't be a total loss, see how *you* would do as a Stooge writer. Here are some more jokes to fill in!

1. This is one of the classic gags the Stooges used again and again when they reached the inevitable ending where they are about to be killed by angry foreigners.
   Executioner: "You may either have your head cut off or be burned at the stake."
   Curly: "I'd rather be burned at the stake. Hot steak is better than a _____ _____."

2. Speaking of cold cuts, Curly got off a rare insult in *Hoi Polloi.* Remember what he told his ugly date?
   "Thanks for the dance—cut yourself a slice of _____."

3. Moe sometimes got the chance to tell a joke. And it was usually terrible.
   Queen: "What were you doing in Paris?"
   Moe: "Looking over the _____."

4. Larry was usually the proud one who said it: "Here we are, three of the best salesmen that ever _____."

5. In *Crash Goes the Hash*, a typical Stooge throwaway:
   Larry: "I been running my legs off all morning 'til the cuffs on my pants are frayed."
   Moe: "_____ of what?"

6. In *Oily to Bed, Oily to Rise, Movie Maniacs,* and a few others, they used this one:
Moe: (to unconscious Curly) "Speak to me kid, tell me your name so I can tell your mother!"
Curly: "My mother _____ ___ _____!"

7. In *Punch Drunks,* Moe uses rare wit with a dame.
She: "I'm in a terrible dilemma."
Moe: "I don't care for these _____ _____ myself."

8. As census takers, the boys had trouble with a woman named Wycoff—especially since Moe kept coughing.
Moe: "What's your name please?"
Lady: "Wycoff."
Shemp: "Excuse him, lady. He's got a frog in his throat from eating _____ _____."

9. The boys were applying for a job in *A Ducking They Did Go.* A salesman asks, "You men ever sold anything?"
Curly: "Why soitanly! Anything we could get our hands on."
Moe: "The gentleman said _____, not _____!"

10. In *Back to the Woods,* the boys used one of the oldest jokes in the world. When the judge shouts, "Order! Order!" What does Curly say?

11. Here's is another lovable wheeze, from *Listen Judge.*
Judge: "What's the matter with him?
Moe: "He thinks he's a chicken."
Judge: "Why don't you put him in an institution?"
Larry: "We can't, we need _____ _____."

12. The boys loved to make terrible puns—even though Moe usually inflicted terrible punishment afterward. Curly mentioned an uncle in Cairo who was a Cairopractor. Then, in the same short, he said he wanted to go to Tunis for some Tunis sandwiches. Shemp had his own favorite. The boys worked as a unit because:
"We're _____."

13. When Moe stooped to similar punning, the results were even worse.
    Question: "Would you fight for this great Republic and . . ."
    Moe: "_____? Nah, I'm a _____."

14. On the map of Europe in *I'll Never Heil Again*, Yugoslavia is spelled slightly wrong. It becomes "Jug O _____."

15. In *Half-Wits' Holiday* Larry got a chance to tell the kind of joke he probably used when he was doing a "School Daze" type classroom sketch in vaudeville.
    Prof: "If I gave you a dollar and your father gave you a dollar, how many dollars would you have?"
    Larry: "One dollar."
    Prof: "You don't know your arithmetic!"
    Larry: "____ _____ _____ __ _____."

16. Moe sometimes acknowledged the boys' rowdy behavior. Here's a one-liner from *Tassels in the Air*.
    Moe: "You don't know us. We make noise stuffin' a _____."

17. Here's one of their haunted house lines. In *Of Cash and Hash*, Shemp is afraid, but Larry isn't.
    Shemp: "Deserted houses? I don't like deserted houses."
    Larry: "Why not? Maybe we'll get _____!"

18. Here's Moe with another one of his simmeringly half-witty comebacks:
    Judge: "Were you ever indicted?"
    Moe: "Not since I was a _____."

19. Curly rhapsodizes in *Yes We Have No Bonanza*:
    "I can see it all now. Me comin' home from a hard day's work. I whistle for the dog, and ____ _____ comes out!"

20. Curly made a drink called a "Nip and Tuck." What happened if you took one nip?

Answers to Chapter 17

1. "Hot steak is better than a cold chop," Curly said in *Restless Knights*, among other films.
2. "Thanks for the dance—cut yourself a slice of throat."
3. "Looking over the Parasites."
4. "Here we are, three of the best salesmen that ever saled."
5. "Fraid of what?"
6. "My mother knows my name!"
7. "I don't care for these foreign cars myself."
8. "He's got a frog in his throat from eating toad stools."
9. "The gentleman said sold, not stole!"
10. "I'll have a ham sandwich!"
11. "We can't, we need the eggs."
12. "We're Unitarians." He said it in *Baby Sitter Jitters*, among others.
13. "Republican? Nah, I'm a Democrat." To which Curly added, "Not me, I'm a pedestrian."
14. "Jug O Saliva"
15. "You don't know my father!"
16. "Mattress"
17. "Maybe we'll get dessert!"
18. "Not since I was a baby," he said in *Idiot's Deluxe.*
19. "I whistle for the dog, and my wife comes out."
20. "One nip and they tuck you away for the night!"

Chapter 18
Photo Quiz II

1. The Stooges clown with Zasu Pitts in the movie *Meet the Baron*. Kids growing up wanted to be just like the Stooges. Who confessed this teenage obsession: "I continued as one of the star comics of the gang, improvised inanities, doing imitations of The Three Stooges."
   a) Arthur Miller
   b) Angela Lansbury
   c) Princess Caroline of Monaco

Courtesy of MGM

2. Shemp was always a real card! In 1944 he nearly formed his own "Three Stooges" with Billy Gilbert and Maxie Rosenbloom. Catch their film *Three of a Kind* to see this trio in action. What did Shemp do to Larry during a real-life card game that was soon adapted as one of the trademarks of Stooge slapstick in films?

3. Here's Shemp again, all dressed up for stooging. Shemp's best-known supporting role was in *The Bank Dick* with W. C. Fields. He played a bartender. What was the name of the bar Shemp owned? Bonus points if you remember his name in the film!

4. Shemp stooged in several Abbott & Costello movies. Which of these *isn't* true?

   a) Lou got mad because Shemp was getting too many laughs.

   b) In *Africa Screams* Shemp got seasick on a raft in a studio lake that held only four feet of water.

   c) Bud did a secret screen test with Shemp for a movie called *Stooge on First*, but decided not to leave Lou after Shemp muffed his lines and kept calling Bud "Moe."

5. An autographed photo from Joe Besser to the author. At
the time it was taken, Joe was a regular on a TV show in
which he played a janitor. Name the series.

6. Joe was friendly with Abbott & Costello. The feeling was mutual, although one time
   a) Joe had to drink a bottle of castor oil during a scene, and Lou substituted real castor oil!
   b) Joe had to pinch Bud in one scene, and Bud got so mad he hollered, "Oooooh! Not so haaaard!"
   c) In a restaurant, Joe suggested that Bud and Lou form a trio with him, and they immediately stood up and began beating him with their T-bone steaks.

7. The boys pose with one of the "outlaws" in their last film, *The Outlaws Is Coming*. The outlaws who antagonized the boys in the film were not professional actors. What were they?

8. An autographed photo from Joe DeRita to the author. Joe made four shorts for Columbia (ironically starting in 1946, the year Curly Howard suffered his stroke). In the short-lived series of domestic comedies,
   a) Joe's hairstyle was similar to Curly's.
   b) Joe wore a wig with bangs, sort of like Moe.
   c) Joe had a normal hairstyle.

9. Moe breaks up the joint on "The Mike Douglas Show."
During one appearance on the talk show, Moe's wife,
Helen, did something special to him. "She hated doing it,"
Moe's daughter Joan explained in an interview with the
author. What did Moe's wife do?

10. Here's Moe, in the photo he sent to the author. Moe was pleased in later life to receive so much attention. But in 1975 he said, "They can keep their star. And I'll tell them where to put it—one point at a time." What got him so steamed?

Answers to Chapter 18

1. a) Arthur Miller. Rumor has it that in the original version of *Death of a Salesman,* the salesman sold "Brighto."

2. Shemp poked Larry in the eyes. It happened during a game of "Klaybash," and Moe laughed so hard he fell off his chair and into a glass door.

3. Shemp played Joe Guelpe, owner of the Black Pussy Cat Cafe.

4. c) Bud never did a screen test with Shemp.

5. "The Joey Bishop Show"

6. a) On the old "Abbott & Costello Show," Lou put real castor oil in the bottle.

7. They were the TV kiddie-show hosts of "Three Stooges Shorts" in various key cities. In the photo they pose with "Officer" Joe Bolton (playing Rob Dalton). Joe hosted the WPIX show in New York for more than a decade. He corresponded regularly with the author, contributing Stooge lore and photos from his collection.

8. c) Joe had a normal hairstyle.

9. She hit Moe with a pie.

10. The Stooges were rejected for a star in the Hollywood Walk of Fame. By the time they got one, the original Three Stooges were all dead.

Chapter 19
Pick Two!

Keep both eyes open: we've already picked two parts of the answer—just finish the job. Go on, get started!

1. The boys were spies in the Confederate army, and they used aliases. They were Lieutenant Duck, Captain Dodge, and . . . ?

2. In *Three Missing Links*, Moe, Larry, and Curly were trying to break into pictures: "We're terrific!" shouted Moe. "We're colossal!" cried Larry. And what did Curly say?

3. In a variation on the above, Moe, Larry, and Shemp were extolling the virtues of their newest invention in *All Gummed Up*. Moe: "It's tremendous!" Larry: "It's colossal!" And Shemp?

4. In *Micro-Phonies*, various unlucky members of high society were treated to a concert given by two Spanish musicians and a fabulous Spanish soprano. Moe and Larry were Señor Mucho and Señor Gusto. Who was Curly?

5. Title of a Stooge short: *Healthy, Wealthy and* _____?

6. This one happened at the breakfast table. Moe ate half an egg and half a slice of ham. Larry ate half an egg and half a slice of ham. Curly was initially "ungrateful" for what he was given to eat. But when Moe explained it, Curly said, "Gee, you guys are swell to me!" What was his meal?

7. The boys were fresh-fish salesmen operating out of a truck in San Diego—which could be smelled as far north as San Francisco. They were Larry Hook, Moe Line, and . . . ?

8. When the boys were working for Ted Healy, they were billed as "Ted Healy and his Racketeers," "Ted Healy and his Gang," and "Ted Healy and his Southern _____."

9. There were three theme songs used by The Three Stooges for their Columbia shorts. "Three Blind Mice" was used a lot. "Pop Goes the Weasel" was also used. Name the third theme song.

10. You'll never find such names for politicians—except in *You Nazty Spy.* The boys were Hailstone, Gallstone, and _____.

11. Like the Ritz Brothers and the Marx Brothers, The Three Stooges were Jewish. Almost. One of the "third" Stooges was not. Who wasn't?

12. In *Three Little Pigskins,* Moe's football jersey was "H202" and Larry's was "½." What was Curly's?

13. One of Curly's greatest routines involved stuffing a turkey—and trying to make sense of archaic recipe directions that most young viewers couldn't figure out either! First step: separate two eggs. Second step: dice two potatoes. In the third step he has a loaf of bread. What's the recipe direction?

14. In *Goofs and Saddles* the boys all play characters named Bill. Curly was "Buffalo Billious" and Moe was "Wild Bill Hiccup." What was simpleton Larry?

15. The Stooges had many slogans over the years. As brave but *Restless Knights,* they proclaimed their motto. Larry: "One for all!" Moe: "All for one!" And Curly?

16. A popular ad slogan for Carnation Milk was "From Contented Cows." The Stooges switched it when they worked for "Carnation Pictures—From Contented Actors." And again, on a tropical island, they got "Milk—From Contented _____."

17. The boys always seemed to fall in love with sisters. There was Tiska, Taska, and Baska, and the combo of Faith, Hope, and Charity. In *Oily to Bed, Oily to Rise* the boys fell in love with three sisters: June, May, and . . . ?

18. Curly cried, "Moe! Larry! The Cheese!" We all know that.

But he never wanted the same cheese! In *Horse's Collars* he was force-fed Camembert, Limburger, and _____.

19. The last two questions involve etiquette. In *Half-Wits' Holiday*, the boys were introduced to Mrs. Gottrocks. They bowed and then offered salutations. Larry: "Delighted." Moe: "Devastated!" And Curly?

20. Later on, the boys were introduced again. This time: Larry: "Enchanted!" Moe: "Enraptured!" And Curly?

Answers to Chapter 19

1. Major Hyde. Don't worry, you get full credit if you answered Major Hide.
2. "We're even mediocre!"
3. "It's putrid!"
4. Señorita Cucaracha. Ironically, the boys lost their only Oscar to a film called *La Cucaracha*. That's a coincidence!
5. *Dumb.*
6. The whole bone and the whole eggshell. As Moe said, "We get half a slice of ham and half an egg apiece. You get the whole bone and the whole eggshell—and you're squawkin'!"
7. Curly Sinker
8. Gentlemen
9. "Listen to the Mockingbird." Oddly, the introduction to the song was used, not the familiar "refrain."
10. Pebble
11. Joe DeRita. Shemp and Curly were Moe's brothers, and Jewish. Joe Besser was Jewish—in fact, his parents were Orthodox.
12. You got the answer at the end of the sentence: "?"
13. "One loaf of bread, well soaked." So Curly punches it.
14. "Just Plain Bill"
15. "Every man for himself!"
16. "Coconuts."
17. April, the best sister
18. Roquefort
19. "Dilapidated!"
20. "Embalmed!"

Chapter 20
O. Yetta Genn

This is scrutiny! Here's another assortment of those gagging gag names that were a Stooge specialty.

1. Nux Vomica
2. Annaconna Pooner
3. O'Brien's
4. Baron of Brains
5. D. Lerious
6. Tarpon Monoxide
7. Cess, Pool & Drayne
8. Mildew
9. Bustoff
10. I. Slipp

a) A Curly monicker
b) A place on a map
c) A doctor
d) A smell
e) Kosher restaurant
f) Crooked investment broker
g) A college
h) A wrestler
i) Lawyers
j) A medical instrument

Answers to Chapter 20

1. b) "Nux Vomica" may sound like a Curly nyuk after too much to drink, but it's on a map. See *You Nazty Spy*. There actually is such a thing—not surprisingly, it's poison.
2. j) "Annaconna Pooner" was a medical instrument in *Men in Black*.
3. e) Curly advertised the place by wearing a sandwich-board sign during a battle in *Boobs in Arms*.
4. a) He was called the "Baron of Brains" (and also "Baron of Gray Matter") in *Restless Knights*.
5. c) A doctor in *From Nurse to Worse*.
6. d) A smell. As inept fish salesmen, the boys discovered that their stock was stinking—especially the tarpon.
7. i) They were lawyers in *Hold That Lion*.
8. g) "Mildew College" is where the boys sang "The Alphabet Song" as Professors Finestein, Frankfurter, and Von Stupor.
9. h) He was a wrestler.
10. f) A crooked investment broker in *Hold That Lion*.

Chapter 21
Ow! Ow! Ow! Oh Look!

Stooge violence wasn't always "for fun." Sometimes the boys really did get hurt! Match the funny slapstick to the real-life consequences!

1. In *Three Troubledoers* Curly shoots a gun that backfires.
2. Moe grabs a rubber hammer and smacks Larry.
3. Moe throws a cream puff.
4. In *Three Stooges in Orbit* Joe knocks into Larry.
5. In *Horsing Around* Joe Besser steps off a wagon.
6. Larry gets hit with a breakaway bottle.
7. A pen is supposed to fly toward Larry on a wire.
8. Curly, frozen solid, is "thawed" on a revolving spit.
9. During a sequence in *Pardon My Scotch*, Moe falls off a table after it's sawed in half.
10. In *The Three Stooges Meet Hercules* Joe DeRita falls off a chariot right onto Larry.

a) Moe gets soot in his eyes and can't work for days.
b) His hand goes into a wooden step and a splinter stabs him. The infected wound keeps him out of work for days.
c) He breaks Larry's nose.
d) His forehead is gashed open.
e) Larry squeals in pain and starts cursing when it sticks in his forehead.
f) Larry suffers a swollen lip.
g) Larry's knocked unconscious.
h) A woman nearly chokes to death.
i) He literally gets cooked.
j) He breaks his ribs and faints.

Answers to Chapter 21

1. a) Moe gets soot in his eyes.
2. c) He breaks Larry's nose.
3. h) A woman nearly chokes to death.
4. f) Larry suffers a swollen lip.
5. b) He gets a splinter in his hand.
6. d) His forehead is gashed open.
7. e) Larry gets a pen in his forehead.
8. i) He literally gets cooked. The effect was like a mild sunburn.
9. j) He breaks his ribs and faints—after slapping the boys, of course. This painful sequence was reused as the opening to *Dizzy Detectives*.
10. g) Larry's knocked unconscious.

Chapter 22
Stooge Utensils

In every Stooge film an innocent object was the cause of incredible stooge slapstick. If you somehow got a chance to visit the Columbia Pictures prop room of the 1930s and '40s, you'd probably smile if you came across these things. All you gotta do is match the harmless prop to the mayhem!

1. A skull
2. A meat grinder
3. A pot holder
4. A sofa spring
5. A lawn mower
6. Wild Hyacinth perfume
7. Bubble gum
8. Yeast
9. A cake of soap
10. Gasoline

a) It somehow gets stuck to Curly's backside at a dance.
b) The boys use it for a machine gun.
c) The boys eat it for dessert, thinking it's cake.
d) A parrot gets into it and flies around, laughing.
e) It makes Curly violent.
f) Curly uses it on his head.
g) Curly thinks it's cheese.
h) The boys overflow the joint by using too much!
i) It gets into a marshmallow cake and bubbles come out of the Stooges' mouths and ears.
j) Larry puts it in a cake and destroys the place!

Answers to Chapter 22

1. d) A parrot gets into it and flies around, laughing.
2. b) The boys use it for a machine gun.
3. c) The boys eat it for dessert, thinking it's cake.
4. a) It somehow gets stuck to Curly's backside at a dance.
5. f) Curly uses it on his head.
6. e) It makes Curly violent.
7. i) It gets into a marshmallow cake and bubbles come out of the Stooges' mouths and ears.
8. h) The boys overflow the joint by using too much.
9. g) Curly thinks it's cheese.
10. j) Larry puts it in a cake and destroys the place!

Chapter 23
Oh, a Tough Guy

Questions to test the numb skull of an advanced Stoogist.

1. In what 1941 movie did this dialogue appear:
   "I haven't seen you around."
   "I ain't been around."
   "In stir?"
   "I was a victim of soicumstance! The D.A. framed me for not knowin' I was guilty! Ain't that a coincidence!"
   a) *Shadow of the Thin Man*
   b) *Fat Chance, Your Honor*
   c) *Dizzy Detectives*

2. In Ireland, Moe learned that in Irish slang "The Three Stooges" meant:
   a) The Three Screwers
   b) The Three Soups
   c) The Three Hit Men

3. In February 1959, the boys made a guest appearance on the quiz show "Masquerade Party." The idea of the game was to have panelists try to identify disguised celebrities. What did the boys masquerade as?
   a) The Gabor sisters
   b) A camel
   c) Buddy Holly, Ritchie Valens, and The Big Bopper

4. What was the name of the first Three Stooges short to be filmed in 3-D?
   a) *Deep Poke*
   b) *We Want Our Mummy*
   c) *Spooks*

5. Who was the first person to poke Curly and Larry in the eyes in a Columbia short?
   a) Moe Howard

    b) Ted Healy
    c) Bud Jamison

6. Which of the following is an 8-mm Stooge collector's item?
    a) A table tennis game between Moe and Billie Jean King
    b) A shuffleboard match between Larry and Ed Asner
    c) A chess game between Curly and Bela Lugosi

7. Which of these is real?
    a) Shemp Hill, North Carolina
    b) DeRita Butte, Montana
    c) Besserville, Arkansas

8. In their first short, *Womanhaters*, the Stooges didn't use their familiar first names. What were their names in this film?
    a) Manny, Moe, and Jack
    b) Jim, Tom, and Jack
    c) Hit, The Road, and Jack

9. According to lexicographer Stuart Berg Flexner, many Stooge insult words go back a long time: cabbagehead (1682), chucklehead (1731), featherbrain (1839), half-wit (1755), and pumpkinhead (1841). But it looks like the Stooges popularized a few! Two of these words were popularized when the boys made their Columbia shorts. Which *didn't* become an insult standard during the 1930s and '40s?
    a) birdbrain
    b) lamebrain
    c) numbskull

10. When Ted Healy was in charge, and Moe, Larry, and Shemp were his sidekicks, Healy was making $1,250 a week. What was the most each Stooge got?
    a) $415 a week
    b) $2,500 a week
    c) $150 a week

11. In the last year of their contract to make shorts for Columbia, what were the boys making?
    a) $850 a week
    b) $2,500 a week
    c) $415 a week

12. "They make themselves creatures of the dustbin, endowed with a restless, brazen, cruel wit. They are funny . . ." This is:
    a) A scouting report handed to Harry Cohn when the boys were considered for Columbia
    b) A review of the act when the boys played the London Palladium
    c) Charlie Chaplin's appraisal in a letter to Groucho Marx

13. Moe wrote the first draft of *Punch Drunks*, the Stooges' second Columbia short. What were the names he chose for himself, Larry, and Curly?
    a) Moe, Larry, and Curly
    b) Bangs, Fuzzy, and Curly
    c) Prune, Broccoli, and Onion

14. What ever became of Ted Healy, the guy who originally slapped around his "stooges" on stage?
    a) He was run over by a pie wagon and retired to become an insurance agent.
    b) He fell overboard during a cruise and was lost— coincidentally, there were three others aboard.
    c) He was beaten up by two guys after challenging them to a fight, and died shortly after.

15. He directed some of the best Stooge comedies under the name "Preston Black." Who was he?
    a) Jack White, brother of Jules
    b) Fatty Arbuckle, who claimed he felt pressed and his mood was black
    c) Moe Howard, who used the alias to avoid a dispute with the directors' union, and to make fun of Jules White

16. Of Shemp he said: "He couldn't work as fast or as good as Curly. Poor Curly was a genius in my view."
    a) Charlie Chaplin, 1971
    b) Larry Fine, 1973
    c) Ronald Reagan, 1947

17. Joe Palma was a member of The Three Stooges with Moe and Larry. Why doesn't anybody remember him?
    a) The short he made for 20th Century Fox after Shemp left and before Curly joined no longer exists.
    b) He was used as an "extra body" for the shorts Moe and

Larry made after Shemp died, but he was used in "long shots" only and his face was never shown.
c) Because Joe Palma is the real name of Joe DeRita.

18. If you joined the Official Three Stooges Fan Club, you'd get a certificate that called you something. What?
a) Five Dollars Poorer
b) Victim of Soicumstance
c) Distinguished Knucklehead

19. One of The Three Stooges' directors was immortalized in 1985 when a rock group took his name for their band. They've recorded several albums. Who are they?
a) Jewels White
b) The Del Lords
c) Charley Chase

20. How long did it take to film the average Stooge short?
a) About 4 days
b) About 14 days
c) About 28 days

Answers to Chapter 23

1. a) *Shadow of the Thin Man*, starring William Powell. The screenwriter must've lifted it as a Stooge tribute— unless he was just a backbiter!

2. a) The Three Screwers

3. a) The Gabor sisters

4. c) Spooks

5. c) Bud Jamison did it, as part of the ceremony to induct them into "The Woman Haters Club." He poked Moe, too!

6. b) Shuffleboard between Larry and Ed Asner

7. c) Besserville, Arkansas, named some 70 years ago by Leopold Besser, one of Joe's uncles!

8. b) Jim, Tom, and Jack

9. c) Numbskull, which dates back to 1855. "Birdbrain" gained fame in 1943 and "lamebrain" in 1934, according to Flexner, a Cornell University professor and noted author.

10. c) Only $150 a week, that chiseler!

11. b) $2,500 for Moe and Larry. Joe Besser, in a separate deal, got $3,500 a week to be the third Stooge.

12. b) London Palladium review

13. b) Bangs (Moe), Fuzzy (Larry), and Curly (Curly)

14. c) Healy was an ornery drunk, but not a good fighter.

15. a) He was the brother of Jules White, and later used his own name, evidently once he'd proved his talents and nepotism was no longer an issue.

16. b) Larry Fine in 1973, in an unreleased videotaped interview

17. b) Shemp died just a few months before the Stooges' contract was to end. So in the remaining shorts Moe and Larry used stock footage of Shemp and hauled Palma around for long shots.

18. c) Distinguished Knucklehead

19. b) The Del Lords

20. a) About 4 days

Chapter 24

"I'll Blow Out Your Brain—Or a Reasonable Facsimile Thereof"

Here are some hard questions—and no multiple choice! See if you can turn up the answers, turniphead!

1. We all know that Curly was supposedly Curly Q. Link, the "missing Link" nephew of Bob O. Link. Listen, detective, what was Curly Q. Link's middle name?

2. What was the immortal slogan of the *Men in Black*?

3. Ted Healy always said this guy was the most talented Stooge. Who was Healy's favorite?

4. In one early film the boys all wore buttons that had the letters "W.H." on them. What did W.H. stand for?

5. Director Ed Bernds said that "The Three Stooges owed a great deal" to Joe Henrie, an "unsung hero." Joe was involved in most acts of violence the Stooges perpetrated, but he wasn't a stuntman. What was he?

6. Parrots have caused lots of trouble in Stooge films, usually by walking into toikeys (i.e., turkeys). When the boys were trying to sneak up on criminals in *Crash Goes the Hash*, they were followed by a noisy parrot. What did it keep saying?

7. The Three Stooges (alias Howard, Fine, and Howard) are officially credited with writing only one Stooge short, their second for Columbia. Name it.

8. According to the *Los Angeles Times* (August 31, 1983), who was the first person to walk on the Stooges' star in the Hollywood Walk of Fame?

9. In 1961, Moe Howard said, "When the man upstairs calls you for the second time, he really pulls you up there." He wasn't talking about death. Quite the opposite. What was he talking about?

10. What was the name of the film the Stooges were making when Curly had his near-fatal stroke in 1946 and had to leave the act?

11. When Curly came back for a cameo role in one of the shorts starring Shemp, what lines did he speak?

12. In July of 1986, *Variety* reviewed a comedy film about the boys. "Take a faulty concept and execute it ineptly, and you have [the film's title]." Name the movie that was considered so bad it was pulled from theatrical release and immediately put on video cassette instead.

13. When Moe, Larry, and Joe DeRita became a surprise success on the "kiddie nightclub" circuit in 1959, what TV host/comedian gave the "new" Three Stooges team their first national TV exposure on his show?

14. In 1983 they were called the "Three Stooges" because they were inept at their sport. "I'm the smart Stooge, I'm Moe," Rick Dempsey rationalized, making the best of it. "I'm Larry, because I'm so goofy," added Todd Cruz. And that left Rich Dauer to be Curly, "because he doesn't have any hair." What sport were these guys playing? Consider yourself a real bright ignoramus if you can name their team.

15. When Curly made his first appearances as a member of The Three Stooges with Ted Healy, he hadn't shaved it off yet. Think before you answer this! What hadn't he shaved off yet?

16. The six "Stooges" were all short. Who was the tallest? Moe, Larry, Curly, Shemp, Joe Besser, or Joe DeRita?

17. In 1935's *Ants in the Pantry*, Moe and Larry were playing cards. Someone said, "Cut the deck," so Curly cleaved it with a hatchet. In 1932 another member of a famous comedy trio had used the same gag. Who?

18. Sometimes Curly rebelled against violence. In *Loco Boy Makes Good* he shouted at Moe, "Don't you dare hit me in the head . . ." Complete the sentence, which explained why.

19. The boys often stayed at classy hotels. One offered "Free Showers." When?

20. *Half-Wits' Holiday* is one of the boys' pie-throwing extravaganzas. Within five, how many pies (or substantial handfuls of pie) struck Moe, Larry, Curly, and the "society" guests at the melee? Remember, we're counting every sloppy splat that scored a hit on someone's head, face, or bent-over backside.

Answers to Chapter 24

1. Quff
2. "For Duty and Humanity"
3. Recede, you guys: it was Shemp.
4. Woman Haters
5. Joe Henrie was the sound-effects man. He loved the Stooges so much he outdid himself finding wacko sounds to go with the action.
6. "Jeepers creepers, what an eye!"
7. *Punch Drunks*
8. Joe Besser
9. He was talking about the revival of the Stooges—their 1960s comeback being more successful than their initial fame.
10. c) *Half-Wits' Holiday*
11. None. All he did was snore and bark as a sleeping train passenger in *Hold That Lion.*
12. *Stoogemania*
13. Steve Allen, who said, "Practically none of the young comedians today do that knockabout style of humor, and we could use a lot more of it."
14. They played baseball for the Baltimore Orioles. At the time Dempsey, Dauer, and Cruz were hitting .231, .235, and .208 respectively. But the real Stooges *knew* how to hit!
15. His mustache.
16. Joe Besser, at 5'6"
17. Harpo Marx. He "cut the deck" with a hatchet in *Horse Feathers.*
18. ". . . you know I'm not normal!"
19. "When it rains"
20. Twenty-two. A later Stooge short with Shemp, *Pest Man Wins,* reused footage from *Half-Wits' Holiday* and added new pie-fight scenes, yielding a total of 30 hits!

Chapter 25
So Ya Wanna Get Rough, Eh?

Even tougher questions for all tomato brains. See if you can take these questions illiterally and get 'em right!

1. When Curly was knocked unconscious, Moe was usually concerned. He'd shout, "Say a few syllables!" And if Curly didn't respond: "Utter a few _____!"

2. On January 4, 1982, this prestigious newspaper ran a headline on the *Front Page* proclaiming, "The Three Stooges Are Riding a Wave of Adult Adulation." They said the "Evel Knievels of comedy" were big business, selling millions of bucks worth of films and memorabilia! Who broke the story?

3. In what part of Brooklyn was Moe born?

4. Some comedy historians believe that Curly's "Woob wub woo" was inspired by a silly comedian who used to go "Hoo hoo hoo!" Name him.

5. Two things brought Curly out of his dementia in *Tassels in the Air*. He was tickled under his chin with a brush. What was the other fuzzy thing he was tickled with?

6. What was the name of the movie the boys did with Dean Martin?

7. Who were "Og and Zog"?

8. In *Rip, Sew and Stitch*, bank robber Terry Hargan had a suit with the initials "T.H." What did Shemp think the initials meant?

9. The Stooges became a hit when a nightclub owner named Paul Bertera booked the boys for kiddie matinees in 1958. In what city did this great Stooge revival begin?

10. When Bud Abbott and Lou Costello split up in the fifties, who did Bud try to get to replace Lou?

11. Why is August 30, 1983, a historic day for the Stooges? (Hint: It took place out on the street!)

12. They were called "The Stooges" and their debut album of violent heavy metal was released in 1969. Who led the group?

13. Which was the only Stooge short nominated for an Academy Award?

14. In a rare literary reference in a Stooge short, a dowager (Symona Boniface) doesn't notice that Moe's just gotten rid of a pie by slamming it up into the ceiling. She tells the nervous Stooge, "You act as though _____ _____ of _____ was hanging over your head." As a kid you had no idea what it meant—how about now? Fill in the blanks.

15. What was the name of the classical tune Christine McIntyre sang, and Curly lip-synched, in *Micro-Phonies*? And who composed it?

16. Jack Kerouac called this Stooge "goofhaired, mopple-lipped, lisped, muxed, and completely flunk." Which stooge was he talking about?

17. Moe used the terms "idiot," "imbecile," and "moron" interchangeably. But they don't mean the same thing. Put them in order of the stupidest!

18. He joined The Three Stooges, even though he had been a success on stage. Dorothy Kilgallen wrote in *Cosmopolitan*, "The next comedian to hit the laughter jackpot of the nation in the manner of Bob Hope and Abbott and Costello is _____." Who drew the praise from Dorothy, and the prediction that he'd "be larger than life on everybody's neighborhood screen"?

19. Gladys George valiantly ran an orphan asylum in the soft-hearted melodrama *Valiant Is the Word for Carrie*. The title was switched for a soft-headed Stooge comedy. What was that title?

20. What was the last film Moe Howard ever made?

Answers to Chapter 25

1. adjectives
2. *The Wall Street Journal*
3. Bensonhurst. Moe said in an unpublished interview, "I'd hate to go back there—not the way it is today!"
4. Hugh Herbert
5. Larry's hair, pulled out in a clump, of course
6. *Four for Texas*
7. The Martians in *Three Stooges in Orbit*
8. Teddy Hoosevelt
9. Pittsburgh
10. Joe Besser
11. On August 30, 1983, the Stooges got their own star on the Hollywood Walk of Fame. If you also knew that Los Angeles mayor Tom Bradley declared it "Three Stooges Day," you're a really smart imbecile!
12. His name sounds like a poke in the eye: Iggy Pop.
13. *Men in Black*
14. "The Sword of Damocles." Moe's response, of course, was "Lady, you must be psychic!" Splat! It was a great moment in *Half-Wits' Holiday*, *Pest Man Wins*, etc. For all you students out there, Damocles was a wise guy who dared to speak out about his king's wealth. The king, Dionysius, had his own way of saying "You're living dangerously." He threw Damocles a party—and Damocles was having a fine time, too. Until he looked up and saw that the king had placed a sword directly over his seat. And that sword was swinging mighty precariously from a fine hair. Make that a Fine hair!
15. "The Voice of Spring" by Johann Strauss, Jr.
16. Larry
17. Medically, an idiot has the mentality of a four-year-old, an imbecile has the mentality of an eight-year-old, and a moron doesn't progress beyond a twelve-year-old mentality.
18. Joe Besser, circa 1941
19. *Violent Is the Word for Curly*
20. *Doctor Death*, in 1973

Chapter 26
E. Nuff, Al Reddy

The last bunch of silly names for people and things! You can do it when you're good and ready. Are ya ready?

 1. Omogosh
 2. Octopus Grabus
 3. No Burpaline
 4. A. Mouser
 5. Watts D. Matter
 6. Hyden Zeke
 7. Davenport Seats
 8. Svengarlic
 9. Old Homicide
10. Slap Happia

a) Manager of Lightning Pest Control
b) Horny emperor
c) A bottle of booze
d) The Emir of Shmo
e) A hypnotist
f) Owner of a detective agency
g) Author of "How to Become a Baby Sitter"
h) College dean
i) The only gasoline containing bicarbonate of soda
j) A place in "Starvania," kingdom in *I'll Never Heil Again.*

Answers to Chapter 26

1. d) Omogosh was the "Emir of Shmo" in *Rumpus in the Harem*.

2. b) Or not 2b? Octopus Grabus was a horny emperor who lusted after redheads.

3. i) It was a gasoline advertised on the radio during *Rip, Sew and Stitch*.

4. a) He was, of course, manager of Lightning Pest Control.

5. h) In *Blunder Boys* he was the college dean, and husband of Alma Matter.

6. f) He owned the detective agency in *Horse's Collars*.

7. g) He wrote the book in *Baby Sitters' Jitters*.

8. e) Svengarlic was a hypnotist. "He'll steal your breath away."

9. c) It was a bottle of booze.

10. j) It was on the map of Starvania, along with Hot Sea, Tot Sea, Cast Toria, Stay Wayoff, Woo-Woo, and the Corkscrew Straits.